Mercantilism as a Rent-Seeking Society

Mercantilism

AS A

Rent-Seeking Society

Economic Regulation

in Historical Perspective

By

ROBERT B. EKELUND, JR.

and

ROBERT D. TOLLISON

Texas A&M University Press

COLLEGE STATION

Library of Congress Cataloging in Publication Data

Ekelund, Robert B. (Robert Burton), 1940–
    Mercantilism as a rent-seeking society.

    (Texas A&M University economics series ; no. 5)
    Bibliography: p.
    Includes index.
    1. Mercantile system—History. 2. Economic history
—1600–1750. 3. Trade regulation—History. I. Tollison,
Robert D. II. Title. III. Title: Rent-seeking society.
IV. Series.
HB91.E4   330.15′13   81–40398
ISBN 0–89096–120–4   AACR2

Manufactured in the United States of America
FIRST EDITION

To our parents

Contents

Preface

A thorough rereading of the classic literature on the mercantile period convinced us that the prevailing paradigm for the period was in need of a major reinterpretation. Recent contributions to the theory of economic regulation and public choice clearly indicated that better explanations than those proffered heretofore by economic historians and historians of economic thought could be made for certain internal and external features of the mercantile economy. The critical literature on the great work of Eli Heckscher, moreover, stressed the "political gap" in his generalizations of ideas and policies. We believe that the "polinomic" study of mercantilism contained in this book helps to complete and establish a theory of policy and institutional change over the "high time" of the mercantile age (1540–1640) in England, while simultaneously explaining the entrenchment of controls in the French economy.

We wish to emphasize several important points about our interpretation. We have not set out to produce a substitute for the classic analyses of mercantilism, such as those of Heckscher or Jacob Viner. These ground-breaking historical works deal with an incredible array of issues, whereas we focus upon the more limited matter of rent seeking and its effect upon mercantile policies and events. There is no substitute for mastery of these scholarly works, and we use them liberally to support or elucidate our interpretation of mercantilism.

Rather, we have sought to refocus the methodological orientation of the study of mercantilism. We view mercantilism as an inclusive system of economic regulation, which was designed to provide revenues for the nation-state and monopoly rents for successful "projectors" of monopoly and cartel schemes. In our study, then, economic regulation refers to the provision of state-sanctioned monopoly rights. We feel that it is by viewing the manifestations of mercantilism over this period in terms of the supply of and demand for monopoly rights and of the forces that impinged on self-interested actors in this process that a more coherent explanation of the evolution of mercantile policies and institutions can be developed. This is the spirit in which we present our analysis of economic regulation in the mercantile economies.

Several other minor points are also relevant. We have, following the classic studies, paid the lion's share of attention to the mercantile economies of France and England, though our framework may be easily applied to other mercantile nations such as the Dutch Republic, Portugal, and Spain. We have, moreover, concentrated on the "early" mercantile period for "testing" our theory about policy developments and institutional change. However, we believe that our methodological framework may be applied to the later period and, moreover, to the emergence of "neo-mercantilism" in the nineteenth and twentieth centuries. Some suggestions for further research along these lines are contained in our concluding chapter.

Many present and former colleagues at Texas A&M University, the Center for Study of Public Choice at Virginia Polytechnic Institute and State University, and Auburn University have patiently and helpfully read portions of the manuscript. A number of these colleagues and critics and reviewers must be singled out for special thanks. For advice on the matters in this book we extend our appreciation to Professors Armen Alchian, Raymond Battalio, Barry Baysinger, James Buchanan, Alfred Chalk, A. W. Coats, Roger Faith, Robert Hanson, Robert Hébert, Richard Higgins, J. R. T. Hughes, Robert McCormick, Dennis Mueller, Douglass North, Paul Pautler, Gordon Tullock, Richard Wagner, David Whitten, and Thomas Willett. We are grateful to participants in seminars given at the University of California, Los Angeles, and Arizona State University and to participants in the Liberty Fund Conference on Ideology, Rationality, and Individuality, held in Blacksburg, Virginia, during the summer of 1980, for useful comments on an earlier version of this work. We would also like to thank the National Science Foundation, the

Center for Study of Public Choice, and the Center for Education and Research in Free Enterprise at Texas A&M University for partial support of this research.

Portions of this book have been drawn from previously published papers. These include: Barry Baysinger, Robert B. Ekelund, Jr., and Robert D. Tollison, "Mercantilism as a Rent-Seeking Society," in *Toward a Theory of the Rent-Seeking Society*, edited by James M. Buchanan, Robert D. Tollison, and Gordon Tullock, pp. 235–268 (College Station: Texas A&M University Press, 1980); Robert B. Ekelund, Jr., and Robert D. Tollison, "Economic Regulation in Mercantile England: Heckscher Revisited," *Economic Inquiry* 18 (October, 1980): 567–599; and Robert B. Ekelund, Jr., and Robert D. Tollison, "Mercantilist Origins of the Corporation," *Bell Journal of Economics* 11 (Autumn, 1980): 715–720. Permission to reprint has been granted by the copyright holders in each case. Needless to say, we are grateful to Barry Baysinger and to the various publishers for allowing us to use these papers in this book.

Naturally, we are responsible for all errors of omission and commission, and we fully expect to be held liable for them. We only hope that our foray into the early mercantile age will help spur further research into the interconnections between positive principles of economic behavior and the evolution of economic policy and institutions.

Mercantilism as a Rent-Seeking Society

1

Mercantilism as a Rent-Seeking Society

> The proposal of any new law or regulation of commerce which comes from this order [merchants and manufacturers], ought never to be adopted till after having been long and carefully examined, not only with the most scrupulous, but with the most suspicious attention. It comes from an order of men, whose interest is never exactly the same with that of the public, who have generally an interest to deceive and even to oppress the public, and who accordingly have, upon many occasions both deceived and oppressed it.
>
> Adam Smith, *The Wealth of Nations*

THE 1930's were the high period for the study of mercantilism. Over this period the classic studies of Heckscher (1934), Viner (1930, 1967), and Cole (1939) appeared, and it is from these studies that the prevailing paradigm about mercantilism is drawn. Within this paradigm there have been two traditions in what (if anything) is presently taught to economists about mercantilism.

By far the dominant tradition has been that propagated by historians of economic thought, such as Viner, who tend to view the history of economic theory as a progression from error to truth.[1] These writers, whose approach is derivative of Adam Smith's famous critique of the mercantilists, have concentrated on an exposé of the fallacies of the mercantilists as expressed by the "central tendencies"

[1]An interesting exploration of Viner's view is offered in Allen (1970). Viner's brilliant study of mercantile trade doctrine first appeared in journal form in 1930 and was reprinted in his *Studies in the Theory of International Trade* in 1937.

in the vast literature of the writers of the period (roughly dated from
1500 to 1776). Among the most often stressed tenets of the mercantilists are the equation of specie with wealth, regulation of the trade
sector to produce specie inflow, and emphasis upon population
growth and low wages.[2] These scholars emphasize the presence of
grave errors in mercantilist logic, errors that were exposed by David
Hume and the classical economists. The primary example of such
faulty reasoning was, of course, the failure of the mercantilists to
recognize the self-regulating nature of the internal and external economy that the "specie-flow mechanism" imposed on the mercantilist
objective of a perennial trade surplus.[3]

A more neglected tradition in the study of mercantilism is that
developed by scholars in the German Historical School and by their
English disciples. These writers argued that mercantilist policies and
ideas were very sensible for a period in history during which the
attainment of state power was the overriding goal of the polity. This
tradition in the study of mercantilism has greatly receded in popu-
larity over the years, so that the principal thing the present genera-
tion of economists learns concerning the mercantilists is not their
historical relevance but their theoretical confusions. This is unfor-
tunate because the positive-economic analysis of mercantile political
economy hinted at by scholars in the German Historical tradition
has never been completed.

[2]A brief survey of these "central tendencies" may be found in Ekelund
and Hébert (1975, pp. 28–44) or in any of the standard manuals on the
history of economic doctrine. The literature concentrating on the so-called mercantile "tool box" is vast and of interest in itself, but, as will become apparent, we strongly downplay the importance of any mercantile theoretical paradigm, however crudely conceived, for the course of economic development.
Much may be learned from this literature, however. In addition to the works
of Heckscher and Viner, see Schumpeter (1954, pp. 335–376), Roy (1943),
and DeRoover (1944). Some of the most fascinating material of this kind
deals with the philosophical and analytical thought of specific individuals; see,
for example, Beer (1938), Morris (1957), Dewar (1965), Chalk (1966),
Evans (1967), and Vaughn (1980).

[3]Keynes (1936, chap. 15) offered a well-known defense of the mercantilists on the grounds that a favorable balance of trade was the only means
available to a country at that time of lowering domestic interest rates and
increasing home investment and employment. Heckscher argued in rebuttal
that unemployment in the mercantilist era was essentially voluntary and in-
sensitive to changes in aggregate demand (1955, 2:340–358).

The central treatment in the literature on mercantilism remains the classic study by Heckscher (1934), the one writer on mercantilism who spans both of the above traditions.[4] Heckscher's treatment, however, while historically comprehensive, is in clear need of a modern reassessment. In the years since his study appeared, economic theory has been expanded to offer extremely useful insights into such matters as political choice (Buchanan and Tullock 1962) and economic regulation (Stigler 1971*b*). It is therefore important to reexamine the historians' analyses in light of these modern developments in order to see if their explanations of mercantile political economy can be improved upon or altered in any important respects.

Methodological preferences aside, all the major students of mercantilism appear to organize their interpretations of the period and its writers around a paradigm that emphasizes certain regulatory implications flowing from a balance-of-trade and specie-accumulation objective. The utility of the specie argument is then further linked to the process of creating and developing the nation-state. This explanation of the mercantile political economy has appealed to scholars because it seems logical and orderly, almost as if the process had been imposed by a benevolent dictator or central planner, whose primary goal was the development of a powerful and effective central state. We shall argue in this book that this is the wrong model with which to analyze historical practices in mercantile economies— that, in fact, causation in this basic paradigm is exactly reversed, and that the balance-of-trade objective was nothing more than the by-product of the interplay of numerous self-interested parties who were seeking rents from monopolization in these early nation-states.

Methodology of the Present Study

In the interpretation developed here, the supply of and demand for monopoly rights through the machinery of the state is seen as the essence of mercantilism. Although the institutional setting was different in these early economies, the general forces motivating the supply and demand of monopoly rights will seem very familiar to

[4]Other important historical treatments of mercantilism are those of Ashley (1923–1925), Cunningham (1968), and Scott (1951).

the modern reader. On the one hand, the state found it efficient to seek revenues by selling monopoly and cartel (guild) privileges. Such revenues supplemented the tax revenues available to the English and French monarchs, and indeed the degree of dependence on revenues from monopolization was very significant in mercantile England and France. During the administration of Colbert (1662–1683), for example, the French state procured roughly one-half of its yearly revenues from the granting of extensive monopoly and cartel rights. On the other hand, the demand side of the market for monopoly rights in these times was inspired by the familiar desire of individuals to procure the shelter of the state from competition and thereby to earn monopoly rents. We have chosen to designate these general activities of monopolization as *rent seeking*.[5]

It should be stressed that our purpose is not to *evaluate* mercantilist ideas from the standpoint of modern economic theory. Rather, it is to *explain* mercantile political economy using positive-economic theory. Our analysis will thus offer an explanation of mercantilism in terms of the costs and benefits that accrued to participants in the processes of mercantile rent seeking. Merchants, monarch, and the public are featured as self-interested protagonists in institutional change. Focusing upon specific examples of rent seeking in mercantile England and France, as well as upon the comparative institutional frameworks in these countries, we seek to explain with our theory: (a) why mercantilism declined in England while being simultaneously strengthened in France, and (b) how an analysis of self-interested forces reacting to the shifting costs and benefits of rent seeking presents a more satisfying explanation for mercantilism and for its course in England and France than the well-known alternative, which suggests that mercantilism was an irrational social order.

With respect to the latter point, there appear to be two views of mercantilism in the literature. The first view, espoused and promulgated to large extent by the historians (with modified and improved versions by Heckscher and Viner), emphasizes mercantilism as a concerted policy of nationalism or state building, stressing an

---

[5]The rent-seeking model will be discussed in more detail in chapter 2. For the basic papers on rent seeking and a number of applications of this approach, see Buchanan, Tollison, and Tullock (1980).

exogenously determined economic policy divorced from the endogenous interplay of self-interested forces. Thus, a policy of taxing the import and subsidizing the export of finished goods is seen as a method of state building, of accumulating specie, or of promoting domestic employment, rather than as the simple product of rent maximization by parties to the resulting income distribution. Mercantile policy, in this view, achieves a life of its own, and the underlying forces producing it (to us, the important matter) remain unexplored and, worse, unexplained.

A second tactic of historians of thought in dealing with the mercantile era, not incompatible with the first view, has been to argue, at least implicitly, that the achievement of laissez-faire was the product of the subjective-philosophical forces of the times. Here we encounter "anticipatory" works on individualism and the natural ordering of economic phenomena, ranging from the writings of John Hales, Locke, Petty, and Cantillon, through those of Mandeville, Hume, and the Physiocrats. Indeed, most common references, following Heckscher's emphasis on "ideas," imply that the intellectual case for free trade (Smith, Ricardo, and earlier writers) made such an impression on effective decision makers that they quickly transformed the proposals of such authors into practice. This view was espoused even before Heckscher (see Fay 1934).

While the latter of these positions may possess some limited merit as an auxiliary, supporting explanation of the mercantile era, the former, in our view, obfuscates our understanding of the period and, especially, of the evolution to laissez-faire in England. While neither position is inconsistent with our own, we reject as incomplete both of these interpretations of mercantilism and of the movement to a free economy in England. Rather, we seek explanations in terms of institutional changes (for example, the growth of the rule of law), which altered the costs and benefits of monopolization to rent seekers. Before continuing with the prolegomenon of our study, a closer look at this method—and that of Heckscher—is warranted.

A broad historical methodology featuring the impact of economic activity on social and political institutions is not original with the present study. North and Thomas (1973), in an important book explaining the rise of Western institutions and economic growth, have identified fiscal policy and alternations in population and property rights as causal factors in the emergence of efficient economic organization. They were preceded in this broad approach by Frederic C. Lane (1958, 1979), who investigated organized violence and its effects upon the economic motives and behavior of Renaissance governments in exacting tribute from merchants for protection. Studies exploring the interconnection of economic activity and social institutions have been very uncommon since Lane's pioneering work, however, and cliometrics has dominated the scene in economic history.[6]

A distinguished economic historian has recently lamented the paucity of such research, arguing that, "if we are to understand economic history, we must be able to understand and to explain the behavior of the government sector" (Davis 1980, p. 3). Davis argues further that a new "polinomic history," blending positive economics and politics, is essential for understanding the central questions relating social and economic structure, in other words, institutional change (Davis 1980, p. 15). Our analysis is clearly conducted in the polinomic method called for by Davis, and our investigation shares the broad methodological concerns of writers such as Lane and North and Thomas. The present study breaks new ground, however, in that economic historians have not considered the role of rent seeking in the process by which institutions emerged within the changing political and economic environment of the mercantile era.

While Heckscher was highly regarded as a scholar, the important critics of his treatment of mercantilism pointed to the utter absence of economic actors in his *chef d'oeuvre*. Economic historians, particularly, were disturbed by his generalized treatment of economic policy and his excessive emphasis on the cohesiveness of mercantilism as an economic doctrine and as a set of unifying policy prescriptions unaffected by actual economic events (Marshall 1935; Heaton 1937; Coleman 1957).[7] Specifically, the historians charged that

[6]Another significant exception is the work of J. R. T. Hughes (1977), who presents a broad and interesting perspective of the impact of U.S. governmental and legal institutions upon social welfare. North's (1979) important and ongoing research on the role of the state in economic history should also be mentioned.

[7]Historians of thought have, by and large and in sharp contrast to economic historians, championed Heckscher's ideational and "doctrinal" treatment. In addition to the literature cited in footnote 2 above, see B. F. Haley's (1936) laudatory and noncritical discussion of Heckscher's book. Heckscher

Heckscher's treatment, embedded as it was in ideas, was practically innocent of all reference to the political process through which the so-called unifying mercantile policies were made. Coleman (1957, pp. 24–25), for example, concluded that the term mercantilism as a label for economic policy "is not simply misleading but actively confusing, a red-herring of historiography. It seems to give a false unity to disparate events, to conceal the close up reality of particular times and circumstances, to blot out the vital intermixture of ideas and preconceptions, of interests and influences, political and economic, and of the personalities of men. . . ." Policy, in other words, could not be treated in a vacuum, nor could the role and interests of parties to the political process be ignored.

Even more recently, Herlitz (1964) noted that Cunningham (1968), Schmoller (1897), and Heckscher ignored Adam Smith's emphasis upon class interests as a dominant force in mercantilism. For these writers, according to Herlitz, "the driving force of mercantilism was the creation of states and the strivings of statesmen after power and authority" (p. 107). Herlitz's general indictment is, no doubt, on the mark, and in this sense our analysis is a return to Smith's original emphasis. One of Smith's principal themes in the *Wealth of Nations* was that mercantilism was equivalent to the demand for regulation and rents by merchants and manufacturers (1937, pp. 250, 403, 420, 425, 460–461, 695–696). Smith attributes mercantile restrictions of all kinds—colonization, restrictions designed for specie accumulation, and so forth—to the self-seeking interests of merchants. Typical of Smith's "capture theory" is the following: "It cannot be very difficult to determine who have been the contrivers of this whole mercantile system; not the consumers, we may believe, whose interest has been entirely neglected; but the producers, whose interest has been so carefully attended to; and among this latter class our merchants and manufacturers have been by far the principal architects" (p. 626). Smith even extends the self-interest axiom to explain the Navigation Acts and colonial policy: "To found a great empire for the sole purpose of raising up a people of

---

was preceded in the doctrinal approach by a number of writers, such as Furniss (1965, originally published 1920), and in a series of interesting papers by E. A. J. Johnson (1931, 1932*a*, 1932*b*). Attempts have also been made to relate mercantile writings to economic conditions (Hinton 1955).

customers, may at first sight appear a project fit only for a nation of shopkeepers. It is, however, a project altogether unfit for a nation of shopkeepers; but extremely fit for a nation whose government is influenced by shopkeepers" (p. 579). Although Smith featured the monarch as a rent seeker, he did not elaborate greatly upon the self-interested role of politicians, though he probably did so more than Stigler (1971*a*) believes. Smith, in other words, would not find the general lines of our discussion very surprising.

While Heckscher, on the other hand, may have at some point sensed the necessity for providing a "transmission mechanism" (as will be evident in our discussion), unlike Smith, he did not or was unable to provide a satisfactory bridge between ideas and events, on the one hand, and mercantile policies on the other. We will show that the application of contemporary positive-economic theory dealing with economic regulation and public choice goes far in filling this important gap in Heckscher's discussion. As Coats (1957, p. 175) remarked almost twenty-five years ago: "Ideas often undergo radical transformation in the cut and thrust of the legislative and administrative process, or when they are subject to the influence of conflicts of personalities and interest groups, and in the study of these processes lies the key to the history of policy."

Internal versus External Regulation

The analytical framework of rent seeking will be applied to the historical experience of internal economic regulation in mercantile England and France. The mercantilist practices of the Dutch, Portuguese, and Spanish will not be ignored where they are relevant to our analysis. For example, we offer a comparative analysis of the efficiency of the foreign trading companies in these economies in chapter 5. The bulk of our discussion, however, concentrates on English and French developments, and we do not present separate discussions of the other mercantile economies. In using the terminology *internal regulation* and in concentrating on England and France, we follow Heckscher (1934, 1:135–325), who devotes two lengthy chapters to domestic regulatory developments in these two economies. We will not ignore external regulation, but our primary focus will be on internal developments. This is obviously the reverse of the usual emphasis, in which mercantilist foreign-trade policies are extensively discussed and analyzed. Nevertheless, internal and external regulation have a dual nature in our approach, which means that both kinds of regulation can be explained by the same model.

Some writers have suggested that dualism of another sort existed among mercantile writers, that is, they often defended free trade internally while simultaneously supporting external controls. That there was a contradiction in English mercantile statements concerning the desirability and efficacy of applications of natural law and free trade is beyond doubt (Chalk 1951; Grampp 1952). The observation that the emergence of a philosophical defense of the domestic market economy occurred in the late sixteenth century is indisputable and indeed is compatible with our position on the rent-seeking process of institutional change. But to defend free trade internally and simultaneously support import or export controls is not inconsistent if both are of net benefit to the individual, group, or political party involved. It may well be that merchants increasingly focused on the necessity of export-import controls after they were constrained from demanding domestic regulation. The process was similar in both areas, although small-number situations and pressure groups may obtain more often among exporters and in export associations. Merchants, in other words, had every reason to support protectionist devices under the guise of state building or any other apologetic they could think of. We simply argue that profit maximization from rent seeking will occur whenever the net benefits of obtaining and granting regulation are positive. Any explanation of the relative intensity of regulation in domestic or international spheres at any given time and under any set of institutional constraints in the mercantile era must proceed along these lines.

The vast differences in mercantile writings and in the policy prescriptions supported by individual mercantilists may be explained largely by the rapidly shifting sands of institutional constraints vis-à-vis all types of regulation and by the particular position and interests of the writer in question. When mercantilism is viewed as a rent-seeking process, moreover, the fact that mercantilism as a system has eluded all attempts at characterization by historians of economic thought becomes readily understandable. To explain the pattern and course of economic regulation in one sector as an expression of rent seeking is to explain it in other sectors as well.

General Trends, 1600–1750: A Synopsis

The period with which this study deals is one that historians commonly label a "transition period." The century and a half from 1600 to 1750 opens at the close of a period of trade expansion and early capitalistic developments and ends before the beginning of the Industrial Revolution, which heralded the beginnings of contemporary society. This period, which historians have only recently been studying for unifying themes (deVries 1976), was generally one of economic crisis and stagnation for most European nations, especially for Italy, Spain, and the largest European power, France, but it was also one of relative development and growth for northern and western Europe, especially for England.

The factors leading to the crisis are numerous, and specific influences are difficult to pinpoint. There were clear and stark population declines in the Mediterranean area and in central Europe over the seventeenth century, although the population of England, the rest of the British Isles, and Scandinavia rose by over 50 percent.[8] The latter development constituted a strong relative gain for northern Europe. Malthusian effects (for example, marriage postponement and epidemics), though probably not a Malthusian crisis, appear to explain these population trends. While a succession of civil wars in France, England, and Spain, the Thirty Years War, and other military confrontations may also contribute to an explanation for general economic depression, they (along with monetary or specie disturbances) cannot constitute a general explanation for the crisis of the period.

[8]Though English population grew significantly over the period, the varying growth rates among subgroups contributed to overall stability. The English peerage grew markedly over the first half of the period, causing social disorders within this class, but, as deVries (1976, pp. 10–11) explains, celibacy, later marriage, reduced fertility, and high mortality after 1675 led to reduced numbers within the aristocracy. The upward mobility and concentration of wealth thus created were powerful forces in promoting a stable English society.

Along with these broad developments, and perhaps as a result of them, the nexus of European commercial and political power shifted northward from the Mediterranean, specifically from Venice, and ultimately to England. The Dutch were an exception to the general rule of economic stagnation on the Continent over the early part of the period, but their seafaring hegemony and nascent capitalist preconditions failed to lead to an industrial revolution.[9]

Clearly, basic economic conditions within the individual mercantile nations must explain differences within countries and a large portion of specific historical events, but such forces have often been the *deus ex machina* of historians in place of explanations of how basic institutional arrangements gave rise to the observed economic conditions. It is our purpose here to study a number of important institutions within these countries in order to add specific content to the often vague notion of institutional change. A cogent explanation for historical developments in the mercantile (or any other) period, in other words, requires specificity, organizing principles, and an appreciation that institutions matter for the course of economic history. This lacuna in studies of the period is the gap that we seek, at least partially, to fill.

Plan of the Book

The plan of the book and some of the highlights of our analysis are as follows. We begin in chapter 2 by establishing the analytical framework employed in the subsequent analysis. As noted above, we call this framework rent seeking. We use this terminology to refer to the activities whereby individuals seek returns from state-sanctioned monopoly rights. Rent seeking as an analytical framework has both

[9]Historians seem to be at pains to explain just why the major site of the Industrial Revolution was England rather than the states of the Dutch Republic, since the Dutch had established an extremely viable preindustrial economy replete with private property rights and cost-saving inventions, especially in the earlier part of the period from 1600 to 1750. Inventions and their exploitation, especially the type of inventions that led to the Industrial Revolution, are the product of a nurturing economic and social environment. The environment created by the vast social and institutional change in England between 1600 and 1750 brought about the necessary preconditions for the Industrial Revolution. Some of these important institutional changes were created by the rent-seeking environment we analyze in this book.

positive and normative elements, both of which are important parts of our analysis of mercantilism. As a form of positive-economic analysis, rent seeking is directed toward showing how individuals behave in seeking rents in alternative institutional settings. What difference does it make, for example, if protective legislation is provided by a unified, powerful monarchy rather than a diverse legislature with competing powerful interests? The normative aspect of rent seeking refers to the social costs of such activities to an economy. As we shall see, these costs will form the basis of a new explanation for a phenomenon that has long puzzled economic historians, namely, why France did not experience an industrial revolution comparable in time and intensity to that which occured in England.

In chapter 3 we apply the rent-seeking framework to analyze economic regulation in mercantile England. The important aspect of this analysis concerns the development of an explanation of why internal regulation subsided in England, establishing a basically free economy. As emphasized above, credit is normally given to intellectuals for this transition, and there is certainly some truth to the adage that ideas matter and have consequences. We argue, however, that poor regulatory design on the local level and competitive rent-seeking forces at the national level were the primary factors leading to the demise of economic regulation in England. This analysis features the struggle to capture the rents from economic regulation that emanated from the king, Parliament, and the mercantile judiciary. We argue that rent-seeking analysis provides a far richer understanding of the rise of a free economy in England than that offered by historians like Heckscher, who basically resorts to hero stories (for example, the common law jurists) or great-men theories in explaining the same historical developments.

The rent-seeking framework is applied to internal regulation in France in chapter 4. Here, in contrast to events in England, we find a vast and very effective system of rent seeking, especially during the administration of Colbert. We show that the rent-seeking model offers a better explanation for some of the various puzzles of French economic development (among them, attacks on innovations and an emphasis on luxury productions at the expense of basic industries) than those offered by the historians, especially Cole's fatuous emphasis on the public-spiritedness of Colbert. Moreover, we argue that the rent-seeking paradigm provides a cogent explanation (namely, an explanation couched in terms of social costs) for the famous puzzle of why an industrial revolution was postponed in France.

In chapter 5 mercantilist foreign-trade and industrial organization will be evaluated. In particular, we analyze the formation and evolution of the mercantile trading companies, especially those in England. Here the rent-seeking framework is pushed a stage further in order to analyze the cartel behavior of these early companies and their relation to the mercantile state. Most importantly, we will discuss how the form of these monopoly enterprises led to the important invention of the joint-stock company. The latter argument supplements the traditional view that an exogenous increase in the demand for capital, facilitated by the contractual provision of limited liability, is the key to understanding the evolution of the joint-stock company. We insist that a more relevant explanation of the invention and rapid evolution of this important contractual form originated on the supply side in the desire of shareholders in the early companies (partnerships) to find a more efficient means of transferring their property rights in these firms.

A summary and conclusion of our analysis is offered in chapter 6. In addition to a summary of the major tenets of the analysis, several concluding points are stressed. First, we emphasize that the rent-seeking framework is not intended as a monolithic theory of all the historical events in the mercantile era. While this model performs very well in explaining certain fundamental changes in policies and institutions, it must be remembered that the policies and institutions we analyze are subsumed beneath a panoply of wars, revolutions, alliances, religious conflicts, colonization, and so on, and that we are certainly not proposing the rent-seeking model as an explanation for all these events. Rather, we view rent seeking as an improved method for scholars to analyze important economic developments in these (and possibly other) precapitalist economies. Second, for the sake of historical completeness, we briefly point to subsequent developments in England and France that go beyond the rather arbitrary end point of our analysis. While France basically returned to variants of mercantile institutions after the Revolution, England experienced an unparalleled era of free enterprise, with only intermittent outbreaks of rent seeking until the latter part of the nineteenth century. Third, and finally, we stress some of the lessons that our study can offer for modern concerns about the regulation and deregulation of industry. England experienced a massive and unplanned deregulation of its economy, and it is important to see if modern efforts to counteract rent-seeking regulation may be improved from this experience (Tollison 1978).

2

The Rent-Seeking Model

> But let us be honest. How much more do we know about
> market process than Adam Smith knew that is of practical
> relevance?
>
> James M. Buchanan, *Toward a Theory of the Rent-
> Seeking Society*

THE central purpose of our model is to explain the historical record
of the mercantilist era as an expression of individual rent-seeking
behavior in a variety of institutional settings. Our positive theory suggests that the evolution of the mercantile central state and its devolu-
tion into modified laissez-faire can be explained as the result of consistent individual-choice behavior under slowly changing institutional
constraints. A blend of methodological individualism and evolving
institutional constraints is central to our main thesis concerning the
rise and fall of mercantilism. If we define the mercantilist era as a set
of economic institutions, then we may explain these phenomena
using the standard theory of choice without recourse to historical
or dialectical explanation. Given the standard and timeless assumptions of individual-choice theory, the rent-seeking model telescopes
into a specification of the constraints that modify economic behavior.
Once the model is developed, we can turn to the historical record and
seek the institutional features that served as constraints to explain
the observed phenomena.

We begin with a brief introduction to rent seeking and how rent
seeking differs from the standard economic analysis of profit seek-

ing. The rent-seeking model is then analytically presented and applied to discuss the rise and fall of mercantilism.

Rent Seeking and Profit Seeking

At the most basic level of analysis we must first define our analytical terminology.[1] In economic analysis the standard definition of economic rent is a payment to a resource owner over and above the amount his resources could command in their next-best alternative use. An economic rent is thus a receipt in excess of the opportunity cost of a resource. It has been observed that it is not necessary to pay economic rents in order to procure an efficient allocation of resources. This argument, however, is based on a poor perception of how the competitive market process functions over time. In this process the presence of rents provides the incentive for resource owners to seek out more profitable (and thereby more economically efficient) allocations of their resources. When competition is viewed as a dynamic, value-creating, evolutionary process, the role of economic rents in stimulating entrepreneurial decisions and in prompting an efficient allocation of resources is crucial. Rent seeking or profit seeking in a competitive market order is therefore a normal, healthy feature of economic life. Over time, the returns of resource owners will be dissipated or driven to normal levels by competitive profit seeking, as some resource owners earn positive rents, which promote entry by competitors into their activities, and others earn negative rents, which cause them to exit from their present undertakings. Profit seeking and normal economic rents are thus inherently related to the efficiency of the competitive market process. Such activities drive the competitive price system and create value (as in new products) in the system.

The task at hand is to distinguish what we mean by rent seeking from profit seeking as we have just defined it in a competitive-market order. To do this, consider a simple example in which the king wishes to grant an enforceable monopoly right in the production of salt. In this case artificial scarcity is created by the state, and

[1]This discussion draws heavily on Buchanan (1980).

as a consequence monopoly rents are present to be captured by monopolists who aspire for the king's favor. Normally, these rents are thought of as pure transfers from salt consumers to salt monopolists. Yet in this example, this can only be true if the aspiring monopolists do not expend resources to capture the monopoly rents. To the extent that resources are spent to capture monopoly rents in such ways as lobbying, bribery, and related activities, these resources are basically wasted (create no value) from a social point of view. It is this activity of wasting resources in seeking transfers that we call rent seeking in this book. If an incipient monopolist hires a lawyer to lobby the king for a monopoly right, the opportunity cost of this lawyer (for example, the contracts that he does not write while engaged in lobbying activities) is a social cost of the monopolization process. Moreover, the deflection of lawyers from productive to wasteful pursuits will generate a disequilibrium in the market for lawyers, with the implication that there will be excessive entry into the legal profession. As will be explained more clearly in the section to follow, these rent-seeking costs of monopoly must be added to the standard welfare-triangle loss associated with monopoly to obtain an estimate of the total social costs of monopoly and economic regulation.[2]

Rent seeking is thus the expenditure of scarce resources to capture a pure transfer. The implications of the economic wastefulness of rent-seeking activity are difficult to escape once the state has intervened in the market system to contrive an artificial scarcity. At one level the king can simply allow individuals to compete for the monopoly right and waste resources through such activities as hiring lobbyists and bribery. This is perhaps the simplest and most readily understood level of rent seeking. At a second level the state could sell the monopoly right to the highest bidder and put the proceeds

[2]The basic paper on the welfare costs of rent seeking is Tullock (1967). Important subsequent contributions are by Krueger (1974) and Posner (1975). See Buchanan, Tollison, and Tullock (1980) for other extensions and applications of the rent-seeking model. It should be stressed, moreover, that rent-seeking activities are not confined to cases in which the state intervenes in the market economy. Imperfect competition among private competitors can evoke rent-seeking behavior under certain circumstances. For more on these cases see Marris and Mueller (1980).

at the disposal of government officials. In this case the monopoly rents will most likely show up in the wages of state officials, and to capture rents at this level individuals will compete to become state officials. This competition might be thought of in terms of excess returns to bureaucratic agents, where these returns are competed away by excessive expenditures on education to prepare for civil service. At still another level, should the monopoly right be sold to the highest bidder and the resources dispersed through the state budget in terms of expenditure increases or tax reductions, rent-seeking costs will be incurred as individuals seek to become members of the groups favored by the tax-expenditure program financed by the monopoly revenues. At all three levels, then, rent-seeking costs are incurred as a consequence of the creation of artificial scarcity by the state, and, as this discussion should make clear, this conclusion is independent of whether the state sells monopoly privileges or grants them in bureaucratic-regulatory proceedings and of the ultimate disposition of any revenues from monopoly creation within the public sector. Rent-seeking costs are incurred in any case, and only the form that such costs take is influenced by how the government transacts its business in artificially contrived scarcity values.

As stressed in chapter 1 and repeated here, like most forms of economic analysis, a rent-seeking paradigm involves a blending of positive and normative elements of analysis. Focusing on the social costs of rent seeking, which we will discuss in more analytical detail in the following section, represents a normative evaluation. Put simply, how much do such activities detract from social product? This normative implication of rent seeking will figure importantly in our analysis of mercantilism, especially of the impact of rent seeking on French economic growth and development during and after the mercantile era. The primary focus of our analysis, however, will be on developing a positive-economic explanation of mercantile rent seeking. That is, what are the factors that determine the nature and impact of rent-seeking activities in the mercantile economies? There are a host of issues to be addressed here, which will be noted as our analysis proceeds. For now, we turn to a more careful analytical exposition of the positive and normative aspects of the rent-seeking model and its relation to our proposed analysis of the mercantile economies.

Rent Seeking and the Rise of Mercantilism

We assume, for purposes of initial exposition, that monopolies are created by the rent-seeking activities of individuals rather than appearing spontaneously or being independently created by governmental authorities. At some time, competition emerges in the production of goods and services, and there exists a state or government having authority to order society as it chooses within the limits of feasible production possibilities (which limits include enforcement costs). In this context we imagine individuals arising who perceive potential gains from procuring monopoly rights to produce particular goods and services. These individuals will attempt to subvert the forces of the market and to monopolize the production of goods and services by having the state limit production to themselves by fiat.[3] The process may be illustrated using figure 1.

The entire triangle, P_cPB, in figure 1 is a measure of consumer surplus in the case of a competitively organized market. Although this surplus accrues to consumers under competition, it is in general a surplus for which no one has a property right. The surplus exists because of technological conditions that preclude producers from perfect price discrimination. The entire area belongs to no one, yet consumers and producers may both attempt to claim it. From the point of view of the contenders for the surplus, the problem is not primarily one of economic efficiency. Incipient monopolists seek to

---

[3]In a mercantile (and in a modern) context, monopoly often means a number of combined producers rather than a single seller-producer. These cartels are simply a formal conglomeration of firms acting as a single monopolist under formal or centralized control. (We shall see in chapters 4 and 5 that French producers—especially of luxury goods—and English foreign-trading companies were organized in this fashion.) In cartels, prices or output shares (or both) are ordinarily assigned to the various firms whose behavior is, in some manner, monitored or policed, and entry conditions must, of course, be conscribed. Cartels may be privately or publicly organized, but there is a keen incentive to cheat on cartel price or output when there is no legal sanction to the arrangement, since each firm has an incentive to lower price or sell outside its assigned market. In sum, most privately organized cartels are unstable and tend to break down over time. The acquisition of public regulation, therefore. is a common and low-cost means used by an industry to organize as a cartel, since the regulatory agency supplies the continuous enforcement of the rules. Through regulation, backed up by legal sanctions against "cheaters," the government may attempt to control such items as entry, rates, or profits.

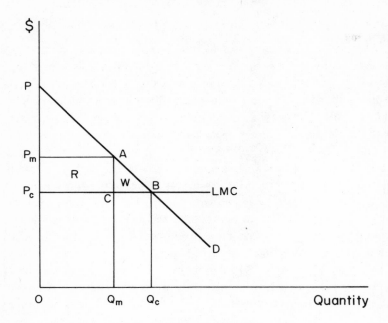

FIGURE 1. Rent-Seeking Model

achieve a position close to P_m, and consumer forces seek a position toward P_c. There are no principles in the theory of choice assigning preference to either position.

The two parties will, in such matters, typically retain brokers (lobbyist-lawyers) to seek a favorable outcome, and each party will devote resources equal to an *epsilon* below their potential gains in their efforts to procure a favorable outcome. That producers are better able to organize and effect the P_m solution is well known, but this is no more undesirable (net of the welfare triangle) than the technological constraints precluding perfect price discrimination. The social waste of monopoly thus involves: (1) the traditional welfare triangle measuring the portion of consumers' surplus that is lost to society because some individuals refrain from purchasing the monopolized output at higher prices (area W in figure 1) and (2) the use of lobbyist-lawyer resources to effect a pure transfer (area R in figure 1). The latter social cost derives from the use of real resources to seek transfers. Such activities clearly add nothing to social product, and the social cost of using resources in this way is their opportunity cost elsewhere in the economy in arranging positive-sum agreements among individuals. Thus, lawyers could be writing contracts rather than lobbying for monopoly rights.

If an incipient monopolist is successful in his dealings with the state, he will be able to impose the classic monopoly solution of $P_m Q_m$ in figure 1, receiving a return on his rent-seeking investment of $P_m A C P_c$, less his lobbyist-lawyer expenditures. With the gain in monopoly rents so depicted, we expect several other features of the rent-seeking model to be present.

First, there is no fundamental reason to believe that only one individual will discover the gains from seeking monopoly rights sponsored by the state. We thus expect numerous aspiring monopolists to compete for these rights, and we assume for analytical convenience that in the long run this competition will drive the returns from using the state as a source of profit to normal levels. Thus, for example, five risk-neutral rent seekers, competing for a randomly awarded monopoly right worth \$50,000, will each expend \$10,000 in lawyer-lobbyist resources in the expectation of obtaining the right, and the \$50,000 in monopoly rents will thereby be dissipated at a social level.[4]

Also, as the above discussion intimates, we expect that those who stand to lose from the monopolization of an activity will have an interest in preventing such losses. Consumers stand to lose $P_m A C P_c$ in figure 1, the rent gained by the successful monopolist, plus the deadweight welfare loss, ABC. In a costless world consumers would invest resources to retain this surplus, and there would be no monopolies because consumers stand to gain more from competitive organization than monopolists gain from monopolies. However, we will exclude such behavior here because of the well-known transaction costs involved in organizing consumer efforts to resist government action in raising prices.[5]

[4]Perfect dissipation of rents obviously rests on assumptions such as competition and adequate information among rent seekers. Without such assumptions rents might not be perfectly competed away, and a variety of interesting analytical possibilities arise. For further discussions see Tullock (1980) and Baysinger and Tollison (1980a).

[5]For further discussion of these points and their importance in assessing the amount of welfare loss due to monopoly, see Baysinger and Tollison (1980).

But what about the remaining party in the rent-seeking model, that is, the state authority holding the power to grant monopoly rights? The interests of the rent seekers are clear, but what are the interests of the suppliers of monopoly rights? In the historical context with which we are concerned, the state may be pictured as a unified, revenue-seeking leviathan, where fiscal needs (defense, court expenses, and so forth) prompted the sale of protective legislation. For example, to "the mercantilist politician, the state was more or less the leviathan, absolute and all powerful" (Heaton 1937, p. 392). In the rent-seeking model this case corresponds to an absolute monarchy in which the royal authority possesses an unrivaled ability to grant monopoly rights. This type of institutional arrangement tilts the bargaining power in the market for monopoly rights in favor of the crown. If enforceable monopoly rights cannot be bought elsewhere in the dominion, most of the consumer surplus in figure 1 will end up in the king's treasury. To be worth anything, however, the king's monopoly rights must be enforced, and since enforcement is not costless, the royal authority will have to spend some of its monopoly revenues on enforcement. Moreover, to the extent that there is competition for positions of royal authority, the monarchy must expend resources to resist bids to take over the royal apparatus. As a part of a cost-minimization strategy for staying in power, it may be efficient for the king to take consumer interests into account to some degree. The absolute monarch is thus not "absolute" in these senses and does not make pure profits from the sale of monopoly rights.

As we shall develop more fully in the next two chapters, the revenue-seeking view of mercantilism conforms closely to European history in the mercantilist era. For example, one historian of the period characterizes mercantilism "as a negative and restrictive factor, which had its principal source, not in any deliberate plan of promoting economic progress, but in the fiscal exigencies of short-sighted and impecunious government" (Tawney 1958, p. lxiv). Heaton (1937, pp. 375–376), reflecting on this appraisal, concurs, adding that "rarely in framing government policy did a government have the deplorable condition of the exchequer far out of mind, and every 'projector' who presented a scheme to his ruler stressed the benefit that would directly or indirectly flow into the royal coffers." Or, consider Heckscher's (1934, 1:178) view: "One of the most important features of economic policy, if not the most important of all . . . [was] what is called in French *fiscalisme*. . . . The state, by its intervention, wanted to create large sources of revenue for itself. . . . The state exploited for its own ends the monopolistic advantages which the gilds had secured for their members or the owners of private privileges had secured for themselves."

In general, then, we may conceive of the situation faced by the monarchical state authority and potential rent seekers in terms of an Edgeworth-box diagram. Given royal prerogative, consumer interests are effectively left out of consideration. Hence, under competitive organization, with the crown at one corner of an Edgeworth box and "projectors" at the other, the solution is off the contract curve, and each party stands to gain from cooperation. The remaining issue is merely the location of the solution on the contract curve. The ease with which mutual interests in monopolization were recognized and realized was relatively great with a unified state authority.

In sum, then, we posit that the pursuit of special favor by individuals was the driving force behind the flourishing rent-seeking activities over the mercantile era. "The incentive rarely came from a whole class, for a class was too unwieldy, too class-unconscious, and too much torn by conflicting factors or interests to have one will or voice. Action came from individuals or compact groups who saw an opportunity to profit by protection or promotion" (Heaton 1937, p. 387). The ascension of mercantilism in the early part of the era is readily explained by the institutional setting facing the participants in the process of monopolization. Since the transaction costs required to seek rents were low with a unified state authority (the monarch), the flowering of mercantilism as an extensive system of monopolization and economic regulation of the economy may be easily explained. That is, since the cost of seeking monopolies was relatively low under absolute monarchy and since the monarchy found it efficient to seek revenues from the granting and enforcement of monopolies (for reasons to be explained in chapter 3), other things equal, more of this activity may be expected.

Rent Seeking and the Decline of Mercantilism in England

At the other extreme from the rent-seeking leviathan were the emerging institutions of representative democracy. The rise of democracy in England was embodied in a struggle over the power to supply legislation in a rent-seeking context. This struggle ultimately led to the demise of English mercantilism because of the profound changes taking place in the institutional environment. Under the assumption that self-interest is independent of time, we argue that an important source of the fall of mercantilism must be found in the changing cost-benefit structure facing potential rent seekers. We have thus far suggested that mercantilism rose because the relative costs of negotiating favored treatment with a state in which authority was vested in a central figure were low. Prior to the centralization of authority, rent seekers had to deal with a multitude of feudal rulers, which caused the costs of negotiating and enforcing exclusive rights to be relatively higher. The correlated rise of mercantilism and central monarchies was thus the result of changed cost conditions, and the fall of widespread mercantile activity in England may be explained as a manifestation of changes in the bargaining environment occurring as the result of political upheaval.

In seeking an explanation for the decline of English mercantilist policies within the rent-seeking paradigm, we follow Hayek (1960) when he notes that "it was finally in the dispute about the authority to legislate in which the contending parties reproached each other for acting arbitrarily—acting, that is, not in accordance with recognized general laws—that the cause of individual freedom was inadvertently advanced" (p. 163). Throughout his discussion of the emergence of the rule of law in England, Hayek stresses that economic freedom came about as a by-product of a struggle for the power to supply legislation. This struggle embodied an effort by Parliament and the common law jurists not, as historians like Heckscher would have us believe, to invoke competition in England in a public-spirited gesture, but rather to share in the monopoly rents being collected by the monarchy. In this struggle several important institutional changes, which dramatically affected relative rates of return to investments in rent seeking by both suppliers and demanders, were introduced unintentionally. Our explanation of the deregulation in mercantile England relies on these changes in costs and benefits.

As the power of the English monarchy declined, the movement to a form of representative democracy shifted the locus of rent-seeking activity to new forums, primarily to the legislature and the common law judiciary, with predictable implications for the decline of rent seeking. For example, with respect to the legislature, the costs of lobbying a representative body for monopoly charters are higher than the costs of lobbying a unified monarchy, because there are multiple decision makers unevenly distributed across legislative houses.[6] The rational rent seeker will reduce his bid for a monopoly right when lobbying costs rise. Moreover, the uncertainty costs facing the rent seeker will rise under representative government. Logrolling in the legislature will mask current votes to some extent, making current legislative outcomes more uncertain. Further, there will be turnover among politicians and uncertainty about the durability of legislation from session to session of the legislature. Also, by the time the English Parliament had asserted its power as the source of legislation, there was basically no prevailing administrative apparatus by which the central state could reinstitute and enforce an extensive system of monopoly rights in the economy. For these and other reasons to be discussed in chapter 3, the costs of seeking monopoly rights rose under early English representative democracy, and the decline of government interference in the economy was predictable because of these higher costs.

With respect to the mercantile judiciary in England, there was an important jurisdictional competition between the common law courts and those supporting the king's interests. The common law courts evolved a doctrine that held that royal monopoly and prerogative were illegal, while the special interests sanctioned by Parliament were legitimate. The king's courts naturally disagreed with this doctrine. The net result was a legal conflict in which one court system would rule that a monopoly right was valid and the other that it was invalid. Under these conditions there was, in effect, no legal basis for enforcing a universally valid monopoly right. This meant

[6]For a proof of this proposition with some empirical evidence favorable to it, see McCormick and Tollison (1980).

that even if a rent seeker could obtain a monopoly grant from the king or Parliament, he had no guarantee that it could be sustained against interlopers. Seeking monopoly through the shelter of the state was clearly going to be a less profitable activity under these circumstances.

As we shall see in chapter 3, a great struggle evolved in England between the king and Parliament and between the king's courts and the common law courts allied to parliamentary interests. This struggle, which had important religious and political themes, was also a struggle over who was to run and profit from the rent-seeking economy of English mercantilism. This conflict over the authority to legislate and to adjudicate legal disputes ultimately meant that the costs of seeking and enforcing monopoly protection from the state rose to exceed the potential benefits for rent seekers, and state interference in the economy consequently declined. A very different cost structure existed in mercantile France, but the monopoly rent-seeking paradigm performs admirably in explaining developments there, too, as we shall see in chapter 4.

Conclusion

The reader now has an outline of what rent seeking means and how we intend to use it in analyzing mercantilism. Our argument is that the rent-seeking model is more useful in explaining developments in the mercantile economies than the usual specie-accumulation interpretation. The rent-seeking model rationalizes the emergence and decline of the social order of mercantilism in England and France in terms of individual behavior in the face of varying institutional constraints rather than in terms of the irrationality or error in the social order of mercantilism. It is. to the development of the rent-seeking explanation of mercantilism that we now turn.

3

Economic Regulation and Rent Seeking in Mercantile England

> It was finally in a dispute about the authority to legislate
> in which the contending parties reproached each other for
> acting arbitrarily—acting, that is, not in accordance with
> recognized general laws—that the cause of individual free-
> dom was inadvertently advanced.
>
> Friedrich Hayek, *The Constitution of Liberty*

ECONOMIC regulation in mercantile England was extensive and was
instituted on both the local and national levels. Yet most of this
regulation disappeared in the period after 1649. By applying the
rent-seeking model to analyze the forces that drove local and national regulations, we can, as noted in chapter 1, elucidate and im-
prove the prevailing historical interpretation of the rise and fall of
widespread government intervention in the economy of mercantile
England.

Specifically, the present chapter analyzes Heckscher's discussion
(1934, 1:221–325) of the rise of internal regulation in England in
terms of how changing constraints redirected resource allocation into
rent-seeking behavior by economic agents.[1] This part of Heckscher's

---

[1]Internal regulation of industry in France, which we discuss in chapter
4, is sufficiently different from that in England to merit separate analysis. As
Heckscher stresses, "On common foundations were erected two edifices which
nevertheless were different in England and France; and the differences are as
important as the similarities. As an approximate generalization we may say
that the resemblances were greater in form than in content, though quite extensive in both" (1934, 1:222).

argument is shown to be consistent in its basic elements with the modern theory of economic regulation (Stigler 1971*b*; Posner 1971; Peltzman 1976). The Elizabethan Statute of Artificers (and to a lesser extent the Poor Law), which was the centerpiece of the regulation of local industry and employment during the English mercantilist era, is also considered in detail. The main point of our discussion is to show that the provisions for enforcement of this regulation by unpaid justices of the peace and the existence of an unregulated sector (the countryside) of the economy had profound effects upon the pattern and durability of this monopoly-inspired system of local economic regulation.

Heckscher's treatment of the relationship between the mercantilist judiciary and the national monopolies created by royal grant is also reviewed and criticized in the present chapter. Specifically, we shall challenge his interpretation of two competing court systems in England prior to and during mercantile times: one (the common law courts) pliant to the special interests related to the Parliament, and one (represented by chancery and the court of the Star Chamber) pliant to the special interests related to the monarchy. Further, we consider how this jurisdictional competition ultimately led to a situation in which regulation to promote national monopoly was not very feasible. Our argument contrasts markedly with that of Heckscher who, incorrectly in our view, saw the common law courts as the repository of traditional free-trade sentiments.

The struggle for the power to supply monopoly rights through legislation is also examined in chapter 3. This struggle led to the Puritan Revolution and to the victory of parliamentary interests in regard to the supply of monopoly rights and sounded the death knell for the rent-seeking society of mercantile England.

After brief consideration of the issue of customs, some concluding remarks are offered on the relationship between our analysis and the conventional wisdom about mercantilism.

The Rise of Internal Regulation in Mercantile England

Heckscher is very explicit about the origin of economic regulation in England: "English municipalities pursued the same ends as the continental, and the forces they set up to achieve these ends were more fundamental than one might think. They bought their privileges, particularly the *gratia emendi et vendendi*, that is, the power over the organization of the market and of industry in general, by monetary sacrifices to the king" (1934, p. 224). There are some important differences in monarchial and democratic rent seeking, but, in a fundamental sense, the old and the modern mercantilism are the same phenomenon. ("Old mercantilism" may be distinguished from its modern variant by the bureaucratic administrative machinery that was attached to the latter in the first half of the nineteenth century in England.) Moreover, in a fully complementary sense local economic regulation served as a primitive manpower policy to forestall the migration of farm labor to the towns. The earliest charters by the Norman kings to boroughs include the power to establish the guild merchant, that is, to restrict entry to those already on the spot and in control. Public-interest arguments, such as the maintenance of quality, were advanced for such procedures, but the self-serving nature of the arguments is apparent.

Economic regulation took a familiar form in English mercantilism—licensing and the restriction of competition among suppliers—but it is important to understand certain critical differences between the conduct of local and national regulation and monopoly and the institutions surrounding them. Local regulation of trades, prices, and wage rates stemmed from the medieval guild system. Enforcement of these guild regulations in the Tudor period prior to Elizabeth was the responsibility of the guild bureaucracy, in combination with the town or shire administrative machinery. Elizabeth attempted to codify and strengthen these detailed regulations with the Statute of Artificers, which outlines the detailed enforcement duties of local justices of the peace, aldermen, and local administrators. Enforcers of local regulations were either unpaid or paid very little for these services, as we shall see, which led to local alignments of economic interests. We will argue that these cabals of interests ultimately rendered the local provision of monopoly rights ineffective.[2]

---

[2]This is not meant to deny that on a number of occasions the general welfare within cities received a voice. For example, in 1690 Elizabeth was entreated by fifty citizens to allow the Dutch bay makers to return to the town of Halstead in Essex County (Tawney and Power 1924, 1:319–320),

At the national level, on the other hand, industrial regulation was created by three means: (a) by statute of Parliament, (b) by royal proclamations and letters patent, and (c) by orders as decrees of the Privy Council or the king's court. Monarchial rent seeking led to monopoly rights in large numbers of national industries, such as those in gunpowder, saltpeter, salt, paper, mineral extraction, and others. The meshing of private interests of monarch and monopolist was firmly enshrined in English practice as early as the fourteenth century (see Power's [1941] analysis of the medieval wool trade). The nature of this alliance was underscored in debate on the issue of monopoly in the House of Commons in 1601: "First, let us consider the word Monopoly, what is it; *Monos* is *Unus*, and *Polis*, *Civitas*: So then, the Meaning of the Word is; a Restraint of any thing Publick, in a City or Common-Wealth, to a Private Use. And the User called Monopolitan; *quasi, cujus privatum lucrum est urbis et orbis Commune Malum*. And we may well term this Man, The Whirlpool of the Princes Profits" (Tawney and Power 1924, 2:270). These revealing definitions of monopoly and the monopolitan (monopolist) remind us that the motives of economic actors are clearly recognizable and have not changed over the centuries. But, on at least two counts, analogies between the old and modern mercantilism within our analytical framework must be carefully drawn. The first caveat concerns the available forms of rent seeking, and the second relates to the supply side of the market for regulation between the two periods.

The question naturally arises as to why the sovereign did not use taxes rather than monopolies for revenue. In the first place there were some early consensual constraints on the English monarch's ability to tax. England's Parliament was already well established when France's first Estates General met in 1302. Maitland (1908, p. 179) reports that by 1297 Parliament had enounced the principle

---

and earlier, in 1575, the city of Norwich issued a litany of the advantages of having aliens in their city, including urban renewal ("Advantages Received by Norwich from the Strangers," Tawney and Power 1924, 1:135). Contractual accommodations between English producers and aliens within a city were also not uncommon. Evidence that consumer interests influence the pattern of economic regulation is quite consistent with the underlying theory, as Peltzman (1976) has shown in a generalization of Stigler's (1971b) theory of economic regulation.

that common consent of the realm was necessary for the imposition of all taxes, save ancient "aids, prizes, and customs." However, these elements of parliamentary consent were not absolute until the revolutionary period of the mid-seventeenth century, which was in large part engendered by a conflict between monarch and the House of Commons over the authority to collect rents to support armed struggles (see Wolfe 1972).

But beyond the consensual constraints, tax collection was a relatively inefficient means to raise revenue for the mercantile central state because the costs of monitoring and controlling tax evasion were high. Barter and nonmarket production were undoubtedly widespread in the agricultural economy of these times, and commercial record keeping was not highly developed for market production. Moreover, tax collectors were susceptible to bribery and not very vigorous because they did not receive the full marginal value of their efforts to collect taxes. These sorts of factors made tax collection an unattractive revenue alternative (at the margin) for the mercantile authorities. Indeed, since most trade off the manor took place in open markets until the end of the sixteenth century, the power to tax these transactions was not, after Magna Carta, within the reach of the sovereign.

Granting monopoly rights as a means to raise revenue did not suffer from the same deficiencies as taxation. Most importantly, competition among potential monopolists revealed to state authorities the worth of such privileges. There were no problems of evasion or guessing at taxable values in this case. Competition among aspiring monopolists yielded the necessary data for revenue purposes to the central authorities, and, unlike the tax collector, the monopolist had strong incentives to protect his monopoly right because he received the full marginal value of his efforts in this regard. Such a system, of course, would be sensitive to collusion among bidders, but there is no evidence that these monarchies acted in such a way (sealed bids, for example) as to make collusion easy for bidders. Indeed, much of the court intrigue of these times, which has a revered place in literary history, may be seen as the means by which the monarch promoted competition among aspiring monopolists.

A second point relates to the nature of the market for regulation. In a modern context Stigler (1971*b*, p. 3) has observed that "as a rule, regulation is acquired by the industry and is designed and operated primarily for its benefit." In both old and modern mercantilism the pursuit of economic regulation is inspired by prospect of a monopolistic privilege sheltered by the state, and, in this respect, the economic logic of both historical episodes is essentially the same.[3] Economic regulation may be seen as the result of a rivalrous process whereby economic interests actively seek the shelter of the state from competition. Modern examples of such regulation are abundant and well documented (Posner 1974). In the mercantile setting the relevant interest groups were local administrators, merchants and laborers in the towns, and, in part, monopoly interests engaged in national and international production and trade. But it would be a mistake to carry the comparison too far. Though the basic natures of the old and modern mercantilism are the same, there are important institutional differences in the constraints facing economic agents within the two rent-seeking environments. The most important difference for the purposes of the discussion here concerns the supply side of the market for regulatory legislation. The national mercantilism described by Heckscher was supplied by a monarchy, and a monarchy represents a uniquely low-cost environment for rent seeking, especially when compared with a modern democratic setting in which the power to supply and sustain regulatory legislation is dispersed among various governmental powers. The consolidation of national power under the mercantile monarchies thus provides a sensible explanation for the widespread rent seeking and economic regulation during this period of English history.

In the course of the discussion, we will see how the struggle between the sovereign and Parliament over the power to supply legislation, and Parliament's ultimate victory in this struggle, dramatically altered the costs and benefits to buyers and sellers of monopoly

[3]A lot of ink has been spilled to try to differentiate the old mercantilism from modern mercantilism ("neo-mercantilism"). The former is seen as a system engineered by a national elite to secure power rather than plenty, and the latter as a system which reflects the increase in the influence of domestic pressure groups in securing policies that have important domestic and international repercussions. We argue that, while there are some important institutional differences between the two mercantilisms, they are basically fueled by the same economic phenomenon—rent seeking. We will have more to say on this matter in chapter 6.

rights in such a way as to lead to a deterioration of English mercantilist regulation. Our analysis will stress that a free economy emerged in England as a by-product of this competition to supply legislation (Hayek [1960, p. 163] briefly makes a similar argument). The emergence of English economic freedom is thus depicted as an unplanned, undeliberated, evolutionary result of rivalry for control of the legislative-regulatory apparatus. Few individuals, and least of all the common man, consciously conceived of the freely competitive economy as an alternative society for Englishmen prior to 1800. Certainly, Smith and others had a vision of a "system of natural liberty" prior to 1800, and they understood clearly how economic freedom increased the efficiency of aggregate production. We argue, however, that these visions were not the force behind institutional change, especially in the period preceding 1750. This change came about as an unintended consequence of human action.

The Enforcement of Local Mercantile Economic Regulation

The legal framework for the enforcement of mercantilist economic regulation on the local level was set out by the Elizabethan Statute of Artificers. The central issues in this section will concern the provisions in the Statute of Artificers for enforcing a nationally uniform system of regulation on the local level and how the means of enforcement affected the pattern and survival of local monopolies in mercantile England. Specifically, the adequacy of Heckscher's interpretations of two key points related to enforcement of the statute will be questioned: (a) that concerning the motives of the local justices of the peace (the chief enforcers) and (b) that associated with worker mobility, given the presence of unregulated sectors close to local regulated economies. Before turning to these issues, however, consider briefly the move to a national system of regulation.

The statute was an attempted codification of older rules for the regulation of industry, labor, and poor relief, with the important difference that such regulations were to be national rather than local in scope. The reason Heckscher gives for the move to national regulation was the enormous increase in wages after the Black Death. He argues that "from that date the regulation of wages ceased to be a local affair and became a national problem" (Heckscher 1934, 1: 226). Heckscher, however, is being somewhat reckless with time.

The Black Death decimated population in 1347–1348, and the Statute of Artificers was inacted in 1563. It is thus very doubtful that much of a link exists between the two events. In our view the more immediate economic reason for the move to national regulation was the inability of the towns to restrict cheating on local cartel arrangements.[4] Towns, in other words, attempted to buy a nationally uniform system of regulation from the king, and local monopoly rights were to be protected against encroachment, especially by "foreigners."

The attempt by self-interested merchants and administrators of towns to regulate economic activity and to prevent "interlopers" on local franchises is evidenced in numerous Tudor documents. The City of London, especially, wished to restrict aliens and foreign technology as inhibitory of town profits.[5] The solution most often proffered was banishing to the countryside aliens or those workers who did not meet "legal" qualifications for trades. Moreover, according to several writers (e.g., Plucknett 1948, p. 32), the royal courts took over the cases involving peasants and workers, not because of the increase in wages due to the Black Death, but as an assertion of royal power over the manor courts. The evidence would thus seem to favor a rent-seeking interpretation of the evolution of a national system of economic regulation in mercantile England. At best the one-time increase in wages at the end of the fourteenth century was used as a pretext for state intervention on the local level.

ENFORCEMENT OF THE STATUTE BY UNPAID
JUSTICES OF THE PEACE

The nationally uniform system of local monopolies was to be enforced by the justices of the peace. As Heckscher notes, "the

[4] It might be asked why violations of exclusion from trades could not be detected and prosecuted by the trade itself. This is because violations had to be brought to trial, and the justices of the peace served as local judges. Rather than waiting for a royal judge to come by the district periodically to conduct trials, the justices of the peace provided an on-the-spot means of prosecuting violations of the monopoly statutes. The benefits of promptly forestalling cheating on cartel arrangements do not need to be belabored.

[5] See, for example, "Complaint of the Citizens of London against Aliens, 1571" (Tawney and Power 1924, 1:308–309). Occupational rents were created, of course, by retarding the entry of new practitioners. We should note here that there were some curious aspects of the pattern of occupational regula-

Justices of the Peace were the agents of unified industrial legislation" (1934, 1:246), and several aspects of this enforcement system are important. A primary feature of the system was that the justices of the peace were to be unpaid. While Heckscher's interpretation of this situation is somewhat muddled, he clearly settles on the view that no pay for the officials led to ineptitude and laziness on their part with respect to enforcement. We argue to the contrary that nonpayment or low pay for justices of the peace established a ripe setting for malfeasance and led to a self-interested pattern of enforcement, one suggesting both sub-rosa activities and selective cartel enforcement of industries in which the enforcers had economic interests.

Although Heckscher does allude to some evidence on corruption, his main conclusion is that there was an inept, rather than corrupt, pattern of enforcement of local cartels:

Justices of the Peace were unpaid. It is not easy to say how far they recouped themselves by accepting bribes. Allegations to that effect were not absent. Thus, in the year 1601 a speaker in the House of Commons stated: 'A justice of peace is a living Creature that for half a Dozen of Chickens will Dispense with a whole Dozen of Penal Statutes'; and there is divers other proof of their corruption. Still writers who have thoroughly gone into the conditions consider this fairly exceptional, particularly in rural districts. *The weakness of the system lay not so much in this as in their indifference and carelessness.* As early as the time of the first great manual to justices of the peace, first published by Lambarde in 1583 under the title of *Eirenarcha*, the complaint was made that justices were scarcely willing to devote even three hours of their time to the Quarter Sessions, where an innumerable number of county problems remained to be dealt with. It was more and more common for justices to meet in public-houses, enjoy an ample repast with alcoholic accompaniment and then carry on without any agenda whatever. Obviously the detailed control demanded by the industrial regulations could not be efficiently carried out in these conditions [1934, 1:246–247; emphasis added].

Heckscher's use of the term *efficiently* is curious in light of modern economics. The behavior of the justices of the peace was quite efficient and predictable, given the constraints imposed by the Statute of Artificers (see Becker 1976). Indeed, modern economic theory leads us to *expect* malfeasance as the predictable response to low pay in situations where there is an element of trust inherent

---

tion in the mercantile economies. See Faith and Tollison (1978) for further discussion and analysis.

in the labor contract (Becker and Stigler 1974). This conclusion follows because the opportunity cost of being apprehended and fired is low. We contend, therefore, that the absence of pay for the justices of the peace led to malfeasance and a predictable pattern of enforcement of the local cartel regulations.

Heckscher may have sensed these points because the implicit pattern in his lengthy discussion of enforcement (1934, 1:246–263) is that the regulations were applied in such manner as to increase the net worth of the officials' holdings in regulated enterprises. A particular manifestation of this type of behavior involved the adage "set a thief to catch a thief." Many of the justices of the peace had interests in the industries they regulated, and this method of garnering income led to a pattern of cartel enforcement that favored the enforcers' holdings in firms. Heckscher put the matter in terms of industries rather than firms when he observed that, "as regards the control of industry itself, there were a large number of people among the controllers who were themselves interested in the particular industries, and of course not in the application of the legal regulations; and to appoint them controllers was to set a thief to catch a thief" (1934, 1:248).

There are clearly numerous ways in which the justices of the peace could increase the net worth of their holdings in the cartel system they enforced. We would expect that the general pattern of cartel enforcement by the enforcers would feature favoritism for the firms in which they had interests—for example, by allowing their firms to cheat on the cartel arrangement while preventing cheating by other cartel members. Consider a possible example offered by Heckscher: "The laws are very significant in so far as they indicate a sincere desire to call a halt to the exodus of industry from the towns and in general to prevent the formation of larger enterprises especially in rural areas. It is true that the resistance was weaker against those powerful urban 'merchants' who employed rural weavers; the law did not place such great obstacles in their way as it did in those cases where the urban masters had to be protected from extra-urban competition" (1934, 1:239).

Independent evidence from Tudor and other mercantile documents helps support the contention that unpaid justices of the peace were not merely indifferent participants in the process (Heckscher's conception), but that they actively and profitably subverted the system. First, let us consider their responsibilities. Though their duties are not spelled out in the "industrial program" endorsed by Parliament in 1559, the Statute of Artificers of 1563 (Tawney and Power 1924, 1:338–350) charges the justices of the peace with the conduct of price-and-wage controls in their jurisdictions (determined at regularly held meetings, in some cases twice a year). They were to issue public proclamations and to hear and adjudicate complaints concerning apprenticeship infractions, worker mobility, wage-price violations, illegal entry and exit by laborers and producers, and so forth (Holdsworth 1966, 1:285–298).[6] It appears, however, that the day-to-day enforcement was delegated to mayors, other city officials, and to a "governour of Laborers" appointed in every town.[7]

Although day-to-day regulations were delegated to a degree, it is nonetheless clear that the justices of the peace were the final authority on adjudication and enforcement and that, early on, enforcement was something less than lackluster. Insinuations that justices' regulations and enforcement were working at cross purposes to the statute may be found in a letter written by a justice (William Tyldesley) as early as 1561. Tyldesley wrote that enforcement of the statutes had been uneven in the shires, fearing that in the end "all will be as good as nothing." But in the matter of evaluating particular regulations, Tyldesley (possibly suggesting conflict of interest)

[6]Notice the parallel between mercantilist and modern economic regulation. Competition from without is retarded by a licensing procedure (apprenticeship), and competition from within is restricted by ensuring that list prices equal transaction prices (wage-fixing).

[7]This is indicated in the following excerpt relating to an assessment of wages and other regulations made by the justices of the peace: "Requiring and straytlye charging and commanding in her maiestie name, All mayours, Bayleffs, constables, officers & ministers, As well within lybertyes as without to se the same executed. And yf eny person or persons shall Refuce to yeld hym selff to thys order, Then the same to be brought to the next Iustice, And to be by hym committed to the gaol, And ther to Remayne for one hooll yere, or els to be send to the cownsell, yf the qualitie of the person do so require. And for the better execution hereoff they ys a governour of Laborers appoyncted in every towne within the iij hyndrythes of Chylterne, Whoo shall sertefye to the Isutices of peace or to the grand Iure every moneth of all suche as he shall fynd obstinate or disobedyent to thees Rate & orders following yf eny be; And that every servand hyred by the weeke or moneth during the tyme of haruist, to take but after the same Rate" (Tawney and Power 1924, 1:334).

wrote: "of Alehouses (which I do thynck to be the verey stake & staye of all false theves and vagobundes) yf one of ij Justices be Redye to put them downe that be to to bad, by & by other Justices be Redye to sett them vpp agayne, yea, and that with stoutnesse, besyde more. So that in Alehouses, they ys littill hope of eny Amendment to be had." And of the wine market: "they that sell them by my lordes servands, or my masters servands, yea, or have suche kynd of Lycenses, & Lycens out of Lycens to them & ther Deputyes & assignesse & to the assignes of ther deputyes & assignes, that no dout off, yf they maye be allowed for good, they have Autoryte to gyve Lycens unto all men whom please them to sell wyne" (Tawney and Power 1924, 1:330–331).

There is plentiful evidence that the justices of the peace were at the very least ignoring their duties, as evidenced by a memorandum on the statute in 1573.[8] But, more importantly, the queen's council provided that high constables (of less authority than the justices of the peace) meet in "Statute sessions" to police them "so as nothinge be by them done therin contrary or repugnaunte to the said Acte" (Tawney and Power 1924, 1:363). It is, of course, most likely that mayors, constables, and aldermen also participated in the self-interested supply of regulation.

That the justices of the peace had acquired a power to seek rents by bribes and side payments was open knowledge by the time of James I. In most revealing testimony before Parliament in 1620 concerning the patent for inns and other local regulations, a member (Mr. Noye) in the Committee of Grievances noted:

There are some patents that in themselves are good and lawful, but abused by the patentees in the execution of them, who perform not the trust reposed in them for his maj.; and of such a kind is the Patent for Inns, but those that have the execution abuse it by setting up Inns in forests and bye villages, only to harbour rogues and thieves; and such as the justices of peace of the shire, who best know where Inns are fittest to be, and who best deserve to have licenses for them, have suppressed from keeping of alehouses; *for none is now refused, that will make a good composition.* There are also some, who have gotten a power to

[8]Section 19 of the memorandum re-charged the justices with enforcement duties, noting that enforcement "is a thinge that is not done in most places, And therefore, the Statute remayneth utterly unobserved, as if there were no such law at all" (Tawney and Power 1924, 1:362).

dispense with the statute of Vagabonds, Rogues, &c. and so make themselves dispensers of the royalties only proper for the king himself.—The like patent is granted for toll, leets, warrens, markets, &c. and set up bills of it on posts, like new physicians that are new come to town, making merchandises of it [Corbbett 1966, 1:1192–93; emphasis added].

Here the local administrators are singled out for rent seeking by the Parliament, with particular emphasis upon the justices of the peace. The issuing of licenses by the justices in return for a "good composition," meaning a good settlement or agreement, could mean nothing if not sub-rosa bribes or side payments.

But there is even clearer evidence supporting our view that low pay (or no pay) for enforcement led to a pattern of selective regulation that favored local justices' holdings in regulated enterprises. Consider the case of a grain-mill patent granted by Elizabeth to Bridgwater in 1585 (Bridgwater was the large port in southwestern England on the Bristol Channel). In the original letters patent:

. . . a clause was inserted binding the mayor, recorder, and aldermen not to allow anyone to brew or sell any beer and ale in the town unless the malt and other grain had been ground at certain water-driven mills called Little Mills. These mills were owned partly by the crown and partly by the Earl of Hertford. Some twenty-five years later, in 1609 or 1610, a prominent citizen of the town named Robert Chute built a horse mill for grinding malt, for his "owne private gaine". Chute was mayor of the town and a justice of the peace, so his duty to uphold the brewing clause of the municipal charter was clear. Yet he not only permitted brewers and others to desert Little Mills for his horse mill, he brought pressure to bear on them to do so. He used the power of his office against some who did not. He had a part of the water supply diverted from Little Mills, and this prevented the two wheels there from turning steadily during dry summers. He had his wife talk with persons who took their grain to Little Mills. Mrs. Chute went to see the son and the maid of a Mrs. Newman who kept a fairly large stock of malt. According to the maid, the mayor's wife had said, "whie doe not your Dame grind her malt at my husbands horsemill. I hope you were well used [there]". Richard Newman, the son, testified that Mrs. Chute had been sharper and plainer with him. She had threatened that if his mother did not take her malt to the horse mill, "Mr. Maior would looke aboute". And, sure enough, he did. A week later Mrs. Newman was arrested and taken to prison. Her husband was fined 20s. at the next quarter sessions. When charges were brought in the court of exchequer against Chute for defying the brewing clause of the town charter, his witnesses defended him on the ground that Little Mills had not a sufficient supply of water to grind all the malt consumed in Bridgwater. As Chute had deprived Little Mills of part of its supply, this was not surprising! Chute's witnesses also testified that the brewing clause had been inserted not for the general welfare of the townspeople, but for the private advantage of John Courte, another prominent citizen, now dead, who had held from the queen a lease for three lives of her part in Little Mills when the town was granted its charter. Courte's son and widow were still getting a profit from this part when Chute built his horse mill [Nef 1968, pp. 52–53].

The incident, taken from the Exchequer Depositions of James I, clearly illustrates the pattern of local enforcement. In the case described, the self-interested justice of the peace succeeded in utilizing his regulatory power in blatant subversion of the patent's charge.

Although it is difficult to find records of illegal transactions in any age, testimony of contemporary observers seems to support a characterization of an enforcement system of internal mercantile regulation in which the chief enforcers were self-interested parties. On the evidence we find Heckscher's claim unfounded that the essence of the pattern of enforcement of internal regulation was indifference and carelessness due to lack of pay. Rather the system of no pay for enforcement led to a pattern of self-interested rent seeking and, by implication, to a pattern of regulation in favor of firms in which the justices of the peace held interests. Heckscher's implicit suggestions, together with independent evidence from mercantile documents, corroborate this view. Indeed, in these ruder times what other goal of regulation could there have been except unvarnished rent seeking? To apply conceptions of the "public interest" to the historical context of mercantile England requires a great stretch of the imagination.

OCCUPATIONAL MOBILITY AND LOCAL REGULATION

There were factors other than unpaid justices of the peace that made the Elizabethan system of local economic regulation difficult to sustain. A more important reason was that it was possible to escape these regulations within England at the time. While the regulations concerning mobility were clearly set out by both the Statute of Artificers and by local justices of the peace, there is evidence that the rules were blatantly unobserved.[9] For example, the "decay, impoverishment and ruin of the cities" allegedly caused by artificers' movement to the countryside was the subject of the remonstrance issued by the queen's council in 1573 (see "Memorandum on the Statute of Artificers," Tawney and Power 1924, 1:353–365). Again, the justices of the peace were to be chief enforcers of the statute, but their actual enforcement was far different than the crown intended.

In effect, buyers and sellers could migrate to an unregulated sector in the suburbs and the countryside, and the existence of this unregulated sector created powerful incentives to destroy the local cartel arrangements in the towns.[10] Considering the difference in internal regulation in France and England, Heckscher (1934, 1:266) notes that "the most vital difference was that many important districts were set free from the application of the statutes in England, while in France nothing remained unregulated in principle, apart from purely accidental exceptions or subordinate points." The effect in England may be seen in the departure of handicraftsmen and industry from the regulated towns in order to produce and sell in the suburbs and the countryside. There is no evidence to suggest that the countryside was "set" free in any conscious, deliberate act of policy,

[9]In 1561, for example, local justices for Buckinghamshire set out detailed regulations relating to mobility: "Item that no laborer do shyfte his dwelling or departt out of hys hundryth, without Declaration of some reasonable cause to the next Justice of Peace, & ther to Receyve lycens, And yf eny do other wyse departte, then the governor ther, or the constables before his departture yf they can, or els immediately after, to make advertysement thereoff to some Justice of peace, whoo shall award a preceptt to fetche hym agayne And to punisshe hym in example of others" (Tawney and Power 1924, 1:336).

[10]Indeed, the memorandum of 1573 permitted the mobility of certain classes of workers upon permission of two justices of the peace, thereby opening up the legal possibility of profitable collusion, though we can find no evidence of such activity. The interest of justices in rural jurisdictions would have been simply to expand the size of the local economy. Since there were no large objects to regulate, expansion of the local economy could be best achieved by keeping labor cheap. Thus, it may have been in the interests of rural justices of the peace to encourage the migration of labor from the cities, an interest which could have been facilitated by collusive arrangements with town justices to regulate wages or to encourage the out-migration of certain types of labor.

but rather this form of avoiding local regulation seems to have been a response to the pattern of enforcement of local regulation pursued by the justices of the peace. Movement out of the towns was simply a way for some artisans and merchants to raise the costs of enforcement above the potential returns.

It should be kept in mind that these moves to escape local cartel regulations did not have to be distant. The suburbs of towns were filled with handicraftsmen who could not get into the town guilds or who wanted to escape their control. Various efforts to bring these cheaters on the local cartels under control proved futile (Heckscher 1934, 1:240–241). It was simply not feasible to control chiseling on the cartel price in this mercantilist version of a widely dispersed flea market. Adam Smith illustrated this point nicely when he wrote: "If you would have your work tolerably executed, it must be done in the suburbs where the workmen, having no exclusive privilege, have nothing but their character to depend upon, and you must then smuggle it into town as well as you can" (Smith 1937, p. 313). Moreover, attempts to bring the activities of rural industry, which moved farther from town, under guild control predictably failed even more miserably (Heckscher 1934, 1:238–244). Cheating on the local cartels thus became the economic order of the day, and the state's lack of success in dealing with these problems is ample testimony to the inefficient nature of the Elizabethan cartel machinery.

Other enforcers had more direct incentives in pursuing such matters as patent infringements, as Heckscher (1934, 1:253–256) outlines. For example, Elizabeth made a practice of granting court favorites the right to collect fines for violations of the regulatory code. Such farming out of tax and fine collections led to a regular pattern of enforcement, for the more lucrative fines came from local patent infringements and not from pursuing the entrepreneurs who fled from town regulation. Given the enforcement system adopted to promote mercantile regulation, then, it is easily seen that an optimal pattern of enforcement, even where there was a bounty system for violations, involved a substantial unregulated sector. The costs and benefits of such a system of enforcement are aptly summarized by Heckscher: "One of them for example wrote in 1618 with engaging frankness that 'having spent a great part of his means in soliciting and seeking after suits, he had at last hit upon one' in the supervision of English lead" (1934, 1:253).

THE DEMISE OF LOCAL REGULATION

A puzzling aspect of the demise of local economic regulation is why the guilds sought a system of regulation that had such poor enforcement provisions. The answer appears to be that the guilds imperfectly foresaw the difficulties of forestalling potential competition both without and within their cartel arrangements. The towns, which were typically synonymous with guild administration, bought their monopoly privileges from the king: "It was precisely these payments, in which the king had a special interest, that gave towns the opportunity of providing a privileged position for their taxpaying citizens and of treating all other people as foreigners" (Heckscher 1934, 1:224). The emphasis in local economic regulation, following the tradition of manorial control, was thus directly aimed at the immediate threat of outsiders, who were not to participate in the city's privileges. The subsequent evolution of effective means to chisel on the cartel, such as moving outside the reach of the enforcement authorities to the suburbs or the countryside, was not entirely foreseen at the time the cartels were established. Moreover, as Heckscher points out, the local guilds were organized in such a way that internal competition was not easily suppressed:

Finally there were several specific features in the English gilds contributing to lessen their effectiveness. One of them was the association of the most varied crafts in one and the same organization—a very common occurrence in England. It is obvious that control could be of little value when entrusted to such corporations. Then there was the Custom of London according to which the completion of apprenticeship in one craft gave the right to practice in any other. In London itself the municipal government attempted to exclude small crafts from making use of this right and succeeded to some extent; but no more than that, at the time of the great municipal reform in 1835, the Custom of London still persisted in more than half the number of cases reviewed. And despite its name, the Custom of London was to be found in a large number of provincial towns. A few examples will suffice to prove how varied the offshoots of this practice could be. A member of the goldsmiths' gild in London called a whole family of stone setters (paviors) to life, all of whom belonged to the goldsmiths' organization. In 1671 these "goldsmith-paviors" were thirty-nine in number, as against only fifty-two stone setters in their own gild. A confectioner who wished to become a freeman of Newcastle in 1685 was allowed to choose a gild, and like the London stone setters, he chose the goldsmiths. Thus the attempt to bind newly accepted apprentices to their own professional bodies was a failure. Above all, the chances of effective professional control [were] thereby rendered very difficult [1934, 1:244–245].

This does not mean, of course, that the guild merchants, or any-one else in the England of these times, actively thought in terms of a freely competitive society as an alternative to the highly regulated world in which they lived. Since they had never known such a phe-nomenon, it is hardly likely that they would have conceptualized in this manner. Rather, we are arguing that the possible emergence of the competitive alternative, brought about by poor regulatory design, could have, at best, been only vaguely perceived by the local mo-nopolists.

Specifically, at the time they bought their privileges from the king, the local guilds were only imperfectly aware of the difficulties of suppressing competition from outside and inside their cartels. Logically, their payments for these privileges would have reflected an estimate of these difficulties, that is, of the expected durability of their protection. As Landes and Posner (1975, pp. 883–885) demonstrate in the context of judicial decision making (to be dis-cussed further below), legislation protecting special interests may have significant present values, even where the probabilities of nulli-fication are substantial. Thus, it was not irrational for the local guilds to have sought monopoly protection in the face of potential difficul-ties of enforcing this protection. Moreover, modern parallels abound. The railroads could hardly have foreseen the rise of intercity truck-ing, and the airlines provide a convenient example of a case where the industry sought a cartel arrangement that, for a variety of reasons (for example, nonprice competition), the government could not effectively enforce.

Our conclusion is that the Statute of Artificers embodied the means of its own destruction. The behavior of the unpaid justices of the peace and the ability of firms to escape regulation were the two major factors leading to its undoing. Heckscher appears to have sensed these points, but he did not examine their implications in terms of economic analysis.[11] We turn now to a consideration of the important part played by the mercantilist judiciary in the demise of national economic regulation.

The Mercantilist Judiciary and the Breakdown of National Monopolies

In the case of national regulation, there were no unregulated sectors, such as the countryside, where competitive alternatives prevailed and undermined the stability of cartel arrangements. Rather, the factors that led to the undoing of national monopolies must be sought in the changing constraints facing economic actors in the rent-seeking economy of England at this time. In this section the role of mercantile judiciaries in the demise of the national monopolies will be examined, reserving for the next section the role played by the struggle between Parliament and the monarchy to control the supply of legislation. Before turning to Heckscher's interpretation of the mercantilist judiciary (and to our alternative hypothesis), a brief discussion of the historical development of the English court system is warranted. An understanding of these judicial institutions is all the more important since Heckscher stresses at the outset of his own discussion that "the greatest gap in the literature of the subject is the part dealing with the practice of the law courts" (1934, 1: 224).[12]

[11]Heckscher's discussion (1934, 1:294–325) of the decay of the industrial code thus tends to look for other causes for the demise of local monopolies in England, for example, the treatment of the guilds by the common law courts. We should comment at this point on the Poor Law and on the so-called policy of welfare discussed by Heckscher (1934, 1:256–261). The justices of the peace were also charged with welfare administration. In the main, although there are some bizzare aspects of Stuart welfare policy, this aspect of economic regulation was not directed at poor relief, as Heckscher argues, but again at cartel formation. Witness Heckscher's (1934, 1:259) account of the regulation of the trading of foodstuffs: "The J.P.s were usually responsible for undertaking by themselves or by means of special juries, a complete inventory of the stock of corn in the hands of producers and dealers and for regulating its sale down to the smallest detail." Pity the poor who were the "recipients" of such poor relief!

[12]Heckscher, as we have (in part) here, relies on the "great work of Holdsworth" (Heckscher 1934, 1:278, n. 59) for his discussion of the judi-

MERCANTILE COURT SYSTEMS

The development of the judiciary in England was a long, complex, and tortuous process. Basically, three common law courts evolved in the period between the Norman invasion and the mercantile era: the Court of King's Bench, the Court of Common Pleas, and the Exchequer. Matters before these courts were essentially civil in nature, and all were initially under the crown's direct control (with the king even rendering decisions in the early period). During the thirteenth through the fifteenth centuries, however, the courts became increasingly independent of the crown, although judges were appointed by the king, who could (at the outset, at least) remove them for any reason.

Although we are not concerned here with the origins and early developments of the common law courts, it is interesting to note that jurisdictional competition among the courts (meaning a direct competition not for litigants but for changes in their charters by government) was vigorous up to the time of the Tudors (Holdsworth 1966, 1:195, 253–255; Smith 1937, p. 697). This may be attributed to the facts that jurisdictions of the tripartite court system were ill-defined and that compensation of judges depended in part on court fee collections (the remainder paid by the crown). More importantly, for our purposes, the functional separation of the organs of government toward the end of the fourteenth century intensified the cleavage of interests between the king's council, the Court of King's Bench, and the Parliament.[13] The council became identified and allied with the

---

ciary. However, as will become apparent, we reach an alternative economic interpretation of the competition between the mercantile legal systems. Although Holdsworth (1966) is a primary source on these matters, the works of Pollock and Maitland (1895), Maitland (1908, 1957), and Maitland and Montague (1915) have also been consulted. Although these authors are less concerned with commercial policy and matters pertaining to grants of monopoly than is Holdsworth, the existence of competing court systems and the existence of a self-interested legal profession (Maitland and Montague 1915, pp. 110, 121–122) are prominent features of their historical accounts.

[13]At this time the Court of King's Bench became simply a common law court. Significantly, however, King's Bench retained, in both style and jurisdiction, traces of a royal court. Holdsworth points out that in its wide powers of control over other courts and officials, and in its wide criminal jurisdiction, it retained powers of a quasi-political nature which came to it from the days when the court held coram rege was both King's Bench and Council. In

executive branch of government (the monarch), King's Bench associated with the judiciary, and Parliament identified as a legislative body (although the latter retained some judicial powers—the House of Lords remains the highest appellate court in England). The separation of governmental functions brought with it a self-interested alignment of concerns between the common law courts and Parliament. Although there seems to have been some question over whether these courts would be attracted to the council (representing the king's authoritarian interests) or to Parliament, Holdsworth observes:

Parliament they [the common law courts] recognized as the body whose consent was necessary to the making of the laws which they applied; while the Council sometimes did or attempted to do things which in their opinion went beyond both the statute and the common law. Common lawyers were an important element in the House of Commons; and the judges of the King's Bench and the Common Pleas were common lawyers similarly educated, similarly employed, often changing from one bench to the other. They were tending to fall apart from that large body of royal clerks who acted in the various departments of government controlled by king and council. It is not surprising, therefore, that the common lawyers came to think that errors in the King's Bench ought to be corrected in Parliament, and not by the Council [Holdsworth 1966, 1:210–211].

Thus, it appears that the alliance between the common law courts and the Parliament began centuries before the mercantile period, by which time the common law courts had cartelized and established firm jurisdictions (and bureaucracies).[14] Equally significant for the matters at hand is the fact that this identity of interests intensified by 1550, owing principally to the presence of a competing legal system, the royal courts, which were most in evidence by the time of Elizabeth I. The competing judicial system, principally representing equity, was based upon a tradition in Roman law (*curia*

---

the future, the possession of these powers by a common law court which was allied to Parliament was destined to be a factor of no mean importance in determining the position of the common law in the state, and in settling the shape of the English constitution" (1966, 1:211).

[14]By the end of the seventeenth century, common law judges had usurped the right to appoint officers of the court, positions of freehold with no duties. Holdsworth reports that these appointments were blatantly venalized by the judges (1966, 1:255).

regis) that crown powers were above normal legal jurisdictions, that is, outside the common law court system (Heckscher 1934, 1:299). These royal courts were found in branches of the Royal Council, in its subordinate court—the court of the Star Chamber—and in other parts of the executive branch of government, the chancellor and the court of chancery. Most of the concilliar apparatus came to the foreground of English political institutions during the reign of Henry VIII (see Elton 1966).

Confrontation and competition between the common law and royal court systems ensued (Hanbury 1960, pp. 99, 111, and 135). Predictably, the intrusion by chancery and Star Chamber into common law jurisdictions via "legal fictions," "writs of errors," and other procedural devices was met by an aggressive response from the common law courts' "cartel." Holdsworth observes: "Towards the end of Elizabeth's reign the [royal] court was attacked by the courts of common law. We shall see that the courts of common law showed at this period a jealousy of all jurisdiction other than their own. They had . . . won a complete victory over the older local courts. They now attacked courts which had greater powers of resistance because they had sprung, like themselves, from the crown. Their theory was that a court could not be a legal court unless its jurisdiction was based either upon an Act of Parliament or upon prescription" (1966, 1:414). Maitland (1957, p. 115) reports that one of the courts of chancery (the court of requests) "perished under the persistent attack of the common lawyers." Clearly, then, the fight over jurisdiction was an important aspect of the struggle between the two court systems during the sixteenth century (Holdsworth 1966, 1:459–461; Plucknett 1948, p. 151). But along with this struggle came an intensified alliance between common law courts and Parliament. As Parliament's power developed relative to that of the crown, it needed support for its legal actions, a support the common law courts were eager to provide. Beyond being peopled by individuals of similar training and interests, the common law courts were also attracted to the interests of Parliament because they regarded Parliament as simply another common law court (the House of Commons could overturn any decision made by a court of common law). Parliament, moreover, could legislate jurisdictional boundaries and other aspects of the courts but was nevertheless dependent upon the courts for the permanence and security of its laws.[15] It is in this judicial environment that the issue of the power to institute national regulation must be considered.

ALTERNATIVE INTERPRETATIONS OF MERCANTILE JUDICIAL COMPETITION

We now turn to Heckscher's interpretation of the complicated and unstable balance of forces within the executive, legislative, and judicial framework of mercantile England. To be sure, Heckscher acknowledges the dual nature of the mercantile judiciary. Further, he displays the common law courts as the repository of the wisdom of the past, operating under the famous premise that they could not create law, only interpret it, and that the law "grows" through such applications of old principles. But throughout his analysis, Heckscher stresses that these courts were the primal element in the cause for free enterprise and against the cause of restraint of trade, the reason being that restraint of trade was not part of the conventional wisdom that guided the common law jurists. Given this assumed free-trade emphasis of the common law courts, how could monopolies be established? In Heckscher's view, the king tried to avoid the common law courts by establishing a royal court system centered in the Privy Council (the court of the Star Chamber), which gave the crown an administrative elasticity to enforce grants of national monopoly. In the competitive struggle between the crown and the Parliament for the right to supply legislation, the common law courts were allied to parliamentary interests against the absolutist tendencies of the crown, and in Heckscher's study the common law jurists thereby emerge as the heroes of the rise of free trade in England.

Thus, Heckscher recognizes a long-standing bond between Parliament and the courts, arguing that "the absolutist tendencies [of the crown] were just as unwelcome to the professional interests of these lawyers as they were repugnant to the upholders of the powers of parliament" (1934, 1:279). But he assigns the high marks for the emergence of liberalism to the common law jurists, and especially Coke, for supplying Commons with the intellectual weapons

[15]Although Coke once argued otherwise (Holdsworth 1966, 4:186–187), Parliament is the supreme legal authority. Common law courts only interpret the law.

for combating royal prerogative. While acknowledging that professional envy and the reduced derived demand for legal services might
have prejudiced jurists against industrial regulation, Heckscher
argues that "the sincere belief in an established legal code" largely
contributed to that effect. Holdsworth, one of Heckscher's principal
sources on these issues, espouses a very similar view, to the effect
that grants by the crown simply got out of hand, becoming objects
of personal profit. Common law and Parliament were thus representing the public interest by taking patent control from the crown
(Holdsworth 1966, 4:346–348). There are many other similarities
between Heckscher's and Holdsworth's treatments of the entire mercantile period, possibly because the latter relies exclusively upon the
historians' (Ashley and Cunningham) "state power–specie accumulation" interpretation of the era, a position not very far from Heckscher's own main theme (see Holdsworth 1966, 4:315–316, 324–
327).

Our view of the judicial situation in England at this time is
substantially different. The main point of our alternative interpretation is that the mercantilist judiciary, whether the common law courts
or the king's courts, was seeking to enforce monopoly rights in output markets and to rescind them in labor markets. Thus, there was
vigorous rivalry between the two court systems to enforce monopoly
rights, the object of each enforcer being to share in the rents from
sustaining monopolies. Uncertainty over the durability of a monopoly right must have become immense in the presence of such judicial
competition. Such an environment in fact leads to the condition that
no monopoly is universally legal: one court could find that you held
a legal monopoly right and the other the reverse.

Before expanding this interpretation of judicial competition in
the mercantilist era, let us take a closer look at Heckscher's contention that the common law jurists were the philosophical agents of
free trade. In evaluating this argument, the first crucial point to note
is that most of this free-trade emphasis was on labor markets. Thus:

The most important application of the discouragement of restraint of
trade in private agreements in England was the struggle against journeymen associations, and later against trade unions, when they went on strike
or in any way collectively came into conflict with the employers. . . . In
England, the measures of the courts and the legislation against this form
of restraint of trade were still further intensified by the application of the

peculiar legal conception of conspiracy. According to this, a form of action which was considered socially harmful became a penal offence if exercised by a number of people in association, even though otherwise it was not punishable. . . . In England the trade unions could be penalized by common law under the legal category of restraint of trade, even after the statutes directed against them had been repealed [Heckscher 1934, 1:281–282].

With respect to output markets the common law courts do not get such high marks in promoting free trade. Essentially, the common law courts and their allies in Parliament competed with the monarchy and its court system in the promotion of national monopoly rights. Thus, the pattern of national monopolies that existed was bifurcated, with some receiving legal sanction from the common law courts and some from the king's courts. This part of our argument requires further clarification, but the following reference to Heckscher will prove useful:

The courts therefore usually held fast to more *constitutional* criteria; that is, they decided according to the legal title which the monopoly could claim and not according to its existence or to its economic character. This gave the common-law jurists greater opportunity of attacking the special interests of their opponents and of preserving the interests of their own associates. There is, however, no doubt that a kind of legal system developed, even though built up on rather formal foundations, and therefore, from the economic point of view, particularly arbitrary. The result was as follows.

Monopolies based on royal privileges were considered invalid. From this followed the further fact that such regulations, issued by municipal authorities and professional associations, if grounded only in royal charters, were likewise rejected as soon as it was believed that they stood opposed to industrial freedom. But this, on the other hand, was far from meaning that unqualified freedom was maintained. First, monopolies created by Act of Parliament were respected; but they played a relatively small part as being rather scarce. Much more important was the second group. All kinds of local rights based on immemorial custom were also respected, and this influenced trade and handicrafts all over the country. . . . The system of royal privileges could not be upheld before the courts. This coincided not only with the political tendency of the common-law courts, but also with their fundamental conservatism. They themselves thought that they were the bearers of age-old legal traditions in the face of the monarchy's revolutionary tendencies. The cry *nolumus leges Angliae mutari*—we will not allow the laws of England to be changed— is characteristic of this attitude [Heckscher 1934, 1:284; italics in original].

The main point here is that monopoly founded on custom or by Parliament was held to be legitimate under the common law, while monopoly founded by royal grant was not. Heckscher sees this pattern of legal choice as an expression of tradition and conservatism, rather than as a convenient prop for legal choice in a competitive legal environment.[16] The matter of monopoly, as such, was not at issue, except in labor markets, and except insofar as members of Parliament were able to convince their electors of the necessity of a "popular" (parliamentary) control over monopoly.[17] The relevant issues concerned the legality of certain monopoly rights and who had the legal right to supply these rights, Parliament or the crown.

The case of Sir Edward Coke is a telling example of the duplicity with which common law jurists approached free trade. Coke—famed as one of the great defenders of personal and economic individualism, as a member of Parliament, common law judge, and attorney general of England—attacked the prerogative of the crown in the grant of monopoly or of special trading privileges to corporations, insisting instead that rights over trade are reserved to Parliament. In the case of *Darcy* v. *Allein*, 1602–1603 (the so-called Case of Monopolies), Coke's decision states that Elizabeth had no prerogative to regulate playing cards as "things of vanity," in part because this would constrain individuals from practicing a trade that had been protected and recognized by Parliament. In other words, only Parliament could act as a regulator. One observer has recog-

---

[16]Indeed, Heckscher argues that the general alternative to monopoly held to be desirable in these times was "balanced oligopoly." Thus, in speaking about the common law interpretation of monopoly, Heckscher (1934, 1:273) argues that "they overlook the whole principle of the system—oligopoly based on a fair standard of living." This concept of competition can be viewed as antimonopoly, as Heckscher sees it, or as an attempt to apply Aristotelian concepts in such a way as to cloak the real economic basis of interest-group activity.

[17]Arguments to the effect that the public interest demanded a transfer of control over economic activity from monarch to Parliament must have been very convincing to parliamentary constituencies. In the debate on monopolies in 1601, George Moore, M.P., waxed eloquent: "There be Three Persons; Her Majesty, the Patentee, and the Subject: Her Majesty the Head, the Patentee the Hand, and the Subject the Foot. Now, here is our Case; the Head gives Power to the Hand, the Hand Oppresseth the Foot, the Foot Riseth against the Head" (Tawney and Power 1924, 2:275).

nized that the authority Coke adduces to support this view is inade-
quate (Wagner 1935, p. 40) and argues further that "in the case of
parliament, Coke makes no attempt to define precisely its power
over trade. He does, however, assert its superiority to the crown in
this respect—not always on very good authority . . ." (p. 36).
Obviously the legitimacy of rent seeking was not the central issue to
Coke; rather, it was a question of which organ of government had
the authority to collect rents. Other judgments of the common law
courts also supported Parliament's power to supply regulation in
output markets.[18]

The judiciary plays a special role in the modern interest-group
theory of government. Landes and Posner (1975) envisage the independent judiciary as a means of enforcing long-term contracts
between legislators and special interests.[19] Their basic point, which
is highly relevant to mercantile England, is that monopoly rights
must be durable to be worth anything to special interests. As we have
seen, conditions prevailing in the English courts at this time led to

---

[18]For a comparable analysis of the English judiciary and Coke, see Leoni
(1961). We do, of course, recognize that the standard applied by the Parliament and common law courts in the mercantile period was not the free-trade
standard in the modern sense. That is, Parliament and the courts may have
regarded the public interest as identical to the removal of patent-granting
power from the Crown. The unintended consequences of the actions of these
two groups, however, brought about an institutional framework wherein free
trade, in the modern sense, was made more feasible.

[19]A recent position taken by Tullock (1978) may be contrasted with the
Landes-Posner position on the vested interests of the independent judiciary.
Contrary to jurists' vested interests in enforcing contracts with special interests,
juries may not have such incentives. If individuals are assigned as jurors to a
case where special interests plead for a rent-seeking (price greater than marginal cost) coalition, they will likely vote in favor of competitive pricing arrangements unless their own special interests are an issue in the proceeding.
During the period we are considering, juries were ordinarily composed of
twelve of the most prominent citizens (large landholders). Juries were thus
automatically rigged against poachers. Most monopolistic activities that were
brought before these tribunals were cases in which an outside monopolist
would argue that a local industry was violating his monopoly. Here, the jury
could easily hold against the outside monopolist, as Tullock predicts they
would. Moreover, it should be noted that the Landes-Posner theory has met
thus far with mixed reviews from the profession. For two papers offering some
empirical support for this theory, see Crain and Tollison (1979a and b). For
criticisms of the Landes-Posner view of the judiciary, see Buchanan (1975) and
North (1978).

great uncertainty over the enforceability of monopoly privileges. The existence of a two-court system, together with the cluster of interests surrounding them, was the underpinning of a very unstable cost-benefit configuration to would-be rent seekers. Grants of monopoly had a very predictable fate in this rent-seeking environment, and, as examples, we may consider medieval and Elizabethan examples of attempted monopolization, most of which failed to provide any rents to the crown.

The Rent-Seeking Process in England: Some Examples

The jurisdictional (court) competition was heightened for centuries before the execution of Charles I in 1649 by conflicts between Parliament and the Crown. The conduct of the wool trade in fourteenth-century England provides a very clear example of this process, which, during the reign of the three Edwards, precipitated an earlier constitutional crisis presaging those of the seventeenth century. The first crisis was over the taxation of wool.

THE MEDIEVAL WOOL TRADE

The wool trade of medieval England was characterized by a large number of competitively organized wool producers and by a smaller number of large-scale producers (largely monasteries), with an even smaller number of wool exporters. An export monopoly was fostered by the combined rent-seeking interests of large merchants and exporters in bilateral negotiation with the king. The mechanism through which these activities took place was an assembly of merchants called by the king as early as the late thirteenth century for the purpose of advice and consent on the matter of export and other taxation, especially on wool. This body, which rivaled the Parliament itself in functions, was willing to consent to taxation since monopoly and other privileges could be exacted from the crown. In short, merchants were willing to accept the costs of taxation and regulation so long as the benefits conferred by regulation exceeded them. In the words of Eileen Power: "What these interests were is as clear today as it was to men of the middle ages. There were first of all the merchants. All taxes on foreign trade were negotiated with them up to 1340, but they were affected by those taxes quite differently from the rest of the community. As long as the tax was not higher than 'the traffic would bear,' the merchants were of all classes least likely to suffer. They might even benefit from the tax if they could get a *quid pro quo* for granting it, such as the removal of an embargo, or the fixing of the staple somewhere where they wanted it to be, or the grant of a monopoly of export" (1941, p. 71).

The ability of merchants to shift the incidence of the wool tax both backward to wool growers, large and small, and forward to foreign consumers (depending, of course, upon elasticity of demand), forced a polarization of parliamentary interests, which came to recognize the deleterious effects of lower wool prices. This interest group was composed of lay and ecclesiastical magnates (the large wool producers) and the knights of the shire, who represented more than a million small freeholders in Commons. Parliament's fight for the abolition of the tax was thus premised upon their objection to the income (rent) reduction from the successful supply and demand for regulation on the part of the king (Edward I) and the wool merchants. Significant constitutional crises that occurred in the 1290's and 1330's resulted principally from a realignment and eventual commonality of interests between Parliament and the merchants. The costs of monarchical regulation (taxes) exceeded the benefits (entry-restricted monopoly) only so long as the king did not impose new taxes on the wool merchants. When he did in fact impose one, because of war and other pressures on the English fisc, wool merchants clearly recognized that the bilateral form of rent seeking was one-sided and unprofitable. Merchant voices thus joined those of Parliament calling for abolition of the tax.

The alienation of merchants was furthered when the king shifted his favor to a group of "rogue financiers" less than thirty in number, who advanced money to the crown on wool granted to him. Power (1941, p. 83) notes that the "king was . . . compelled to impose an embargo on general export for a time (sometimes a whole year) in order to enable his financiers to dispose of the wool on his behalf. And every time this happened a virtual monopoly of a financial group was established." The result was the dissolution of the larger group of merchant exporters, with those "shut out" becoming disposed (in their self-interest) to urge Parliament to impose constraints on the king.

Though Parliament was unsuccessful in obtaining abolition of the periodically imposed ("extraordinary") wool tax ("maltote"), the increased demand of the sovereign for funds at the outbreak of the Hundred Years War (1337) was met by a tax, but with domestic price controls on wool as quid pro quo. At this point the wool merchants were still sanguine about the export-monopoly franchise since the prospect of passing the tax forward still existed (Power 1941, p. 81). In 1350 Parliament finally gave up on the issue of abolishing the tax but got control over it and converted it into a parliamentary subsidy for specified time periods. A quasi-monopoly of the wool trade, the English Company of the Staple) remained, and, as Power reported, "it is by virtue of this monopoly alone that they were able to shoulder the subsidy" (p. 85), the latter contingent on the will and consent of Parliament.[20]

The pattern and effects of mercantile monarchy, as developed in our theory of rent seeking, may be clearly discerned in the early history of the medieval wool trade. Again and again in the mercantile period—and most significantly in the sixteenth and seventeenth centuries—Parliament was strengthened to limit and oppose the ability of the crown to supply regulation. In England the rent-seeking proclivities of the crown were strengthened by a legislative constraint on its possible revenue. Extraordinary expenditures, which arose with ever-increasing frequency in order to conduct wars, meant that English monarchs were always in need of funds. (The French crown was often similarly situated, but it did not face the same con-

[20]Again Power's (1941, pp. 84–85) analysis of the situation is instructive. She notes that "it is—in my view—a mistake to regard parliament and the assembly of merchants as rival bodies competing for survival and each representing a different conception of social orders—the estates of the realm *versus* the estate of merchants. They were essentially the representative assemblies of different economic interests. The assembly of merchants did not represent all the merchants, and parliament did not represent all the estates minus the merchants. They were two economic groups—on the one side wool merchants and on the other side the other interests, including the growers and those merchants who were not wool merchants, that is the great bulk of the burgesses. If finally the separate existence of an assembly of wool merchants came to an end (though, incidentally, it continued to function spasmodically for purposes other than taxation), it was not because the estate of merchants had ceased to exist, but because the separate and united attention of the wool merchants to the one important economic issue, that of taxation, ceased to function. It was no longer separate and certainly no longer united."

straints, as we shall see in chapter 4.) The crown's reaction to this situation was initially to offer special favors, monopoly-entry control, to growing national industries (large exporters were often fewer in number, were organized with lower transactions costs, and were more easily controlled), who, in return, submitted to taxation.

Reactions to this state of affairs were twofold and eventually brought about the decline of monarchial rent seeking and an increase in costs to legislative supply of regulation. First, Parliament, which represented "society's" and, ultimately, merchants' interests, grew restive at the monarchial rent-seeking franchises. As the mercantile period wore on, this restiveness became more pronounced. Secondly, and more importantly perhaps, the absolutist aspects of the English monarchy were more and more eroded with the aid and action of the merchant classes themselves. A high degree of uncertainty crept in as merchants grew wary of the net benefits of a regulatory alliance with the king. Specifically, this uncertainty of benefits drove merchants to support the interests of Parliament, which reduced the powers of the monarch in economic as well as legal and religious matters. In this manner it may be said that the caprice of monarchical power, which led to uncertainty among merchants, landowners, and freeholders, resulted in the emergent constitutional solution of the late sixteenth and seventeenth centuries.

LATER EXAMPLES OF RENT SEEKING

We must now amplify and further illustrate the pattern of rent seeking discerned in the medieval wool trade and described by our theory. Here we focus upon a "high period of mercantile monarchy," followed by its fall in 1640 or so. Roughly, our treatment extends from the reign of Elizabeth I, the last Tudor monarch, through those of James I and Charles I, the first two Stuarts.

The constraints on regulatory supply and demand between the death of Henry VIII (1547) and the execution of Charles I (1649) were in kind very much like those described for the earlier period. The monarch was still dependent upon the consent of the taxed in order to obtain revenue. He still depended, in other words, upon the good will and self-interest of the wealthy gentry and landowners in order to function, especially when he had to meet "extraordinary" expenses. Over this period, the three major checks upon the crown's power and rent-seeking activities were (a) private local interests composed of increasingly wealthy city merchants and magistrates, (b) common law courts, and (c) the House of Commons. The latter two institutions were increasingly representative of and peopled by the wealthy merchants from whom the king wished to extract rents.[21]

The actual means of rent seeking and the king's ability to enforce it were likewise in transition, being eroded by self-interested forces and constitutional law. As indicated earlier in this chapter, the crown had to depend upon three means of imposing industrial regulation: (1) enactment of regulation by statutes of Parliament, (2) royal proclamations and letters patent, and (3) orders of privy council or decrees instituted by privy council sitting in Star Chamber (the king's court). Developments of the period 1547–1640 may be characterized as leading to the utter supremacy of Parliament in the imposition of regulation. The concept of the "crown in council" as ultimate authority—the great Tudor contribution to administrative government—was also swept away by the events of these years, though the conciliar form of executive administration survives and indeed is enshrined in the forms of most contemporary representative governments (see Elton 1966). During this period, self-interested forces successfully opposed every attempt of the crown to impose and enforce industrial regulation. We now turn to a few examples of these forces.

ELIZABETHAN RENT SEEKING

The reign of Elizabeth I (1558–1603) is regarded by many as the high time of successful mercantile policy. Historical facts do not appear to justify this view, however. To echo a modern directive,

---

[21]Here we must emphasize that we are not trying to explain the decline of rent seeking solely in terms of the rise of constitutional democracy, though we argue that it is a major causal factor in explaining mercantile policies. Technological growth and an emergent factory system, a familiar *deus ex machina*, may have (for example) fostered powerful interests (such as wool buyers or household producers), which arose to compete with the large wool producers and exporters for rents in Parliament, thereby dissipating them. North and Thomas (1973) emphasize still other changes as the grounds of economic development and the emergence of property rights. While their arguments concern somewhat more fundamental causal features of development, they do not emphasize, as we do here, the role of rent seeking in the decline of mercantilism.

regulation should not be judged on the basis of its aim or intent, but on grounds of its effects (Stigler and Friedland 1962). The fact is that Elizabeth opened her reign with a great deal of patent granting and lusty rent seeking from industry but closed it meekly admitting that patent monopoly was a dangerous innovation contrary to common law. Consider the following examples.

The queen claimed regalian rights to the manufacture of saltpeter and gunpowder (on grounds of national defense) and granted a monopoly to George and John Evlyn. The Evlyn family enjoyed lucrative benefits from the rent splitting for almost fifty years (until 1635).[22] But steady counteraction ensued on the part of merchants and the courts, dating from the initial award, which finally brought the monopoly restrictions down. Subsequently, the manufacture of both saltpeter and gunpowder became the object of open competition.

Examples of the attempts to monopolize other industries over the period and the failures of the state may be multiplied. The rights to royalties from the monopolization of ores other than gold and silver were shorn from the crown in a court decision of 1566, which limited regalian rights to gold and silver only (none in England). Self-interested officials charged with dealing with mining leases on royal lands were not above the lure of pecuniary aggrandizement. Thus, Nef notes: "Even in royal manors and forests, where the king or queen like any other landlord owned the minerals and appointed special officials to deal with their mining lessees, these officials, like the justices of the peace and the sheriffs, were always local men who were frequently more mindful of the wishes of their rich neighbors with investments in the mines than of the interests of their royal masters" (1968, p. 101).

Attempts by Elizabeth to duplicate the French king's successful and lucrative salt tax (the *gabelle*) were also doomed to failure. In 1564 she tried to establish a patent monopoly in salt, but the patentees gave up within five years, leaving huge salt pans rusting on the

[22]It is interesting that, though Elizabeth claimed regalian rights on grounds of national defense, she stood to gain monetarily by the conditions of the rent split. All unused gunpowder could be sold by her at a profit to both domestic and foreign consumers. Since by law she claimed all of Evlyn's output, a time of peace meant pure profit to Elizabeth.

English coast. To rub salt in these wounds, private capitalists, *sans* grant, entered the industry and profitably produced and marketed salt over the next three decades in spite of repeated attempts by the crown to reestablish monopoly rights. A further example of the futile attempt of Elizabeth's councillors to grant monopolies to court favorites was the paper monopoly, originally granted to John Spilman in 1588. Spilman claimed to have a new process for producing white paper. In practice, patents issued to protect a new process or invention were ordinarily unopposed by Commons and the courts and were often extended to enable patentees to "engulf" closely related products. Such was the case with Spilman, who in 1597 was granted a monopoly over all kinds of paper. The monopoly privileges were not enforceable, however, and within six years Spilman had to rest content with "such a share of the expanding market for paper as the efficiency of his machinery, the skill of his workmen, and the situation of his mills enabled him to command" (Nef 1968, p. 106). Elizabeth's luckless adventures into monopoly-creating, rent-seeking activities ended in 1603 (the year of her death), when she personally declared with respect to a proposed monopoly on playing cards that such patents were contrary to common law.

POST-ELIZABETHAN RENT SEEKING

What was voiced opposition to crown attempts to monopolize during Elizabeth's era became shouts of protest, culminating in civil war, during the next forty years. As a general rule it may be said that after 1603—in spite of even more vigorous attempts by James I and Charles I to establish monopolies—no acts establishing national monopolies were enforceable if they interfered with the profits of merchants and the interests of those represented by Commons and the courts. Here we find the de facto end of monarchial mercantilism, when, in the context of expanding industries, the net benefit from no regulation outweighed the net benefit from crown protection. The demand for regulation may be said to have been reduced by rising franchise costs (taxes), together with the vicissitudes and uncertainties of crown supply of regulation. Potential competition for investment outlets and political pressures upon Commons by affected merchants must have greatly increased the uncertainty of gains from monarchially created monopoly.

Both James I and Charles I tried to revive Elizabeth's early policy of patent grants as sources of revenue, but both met with very limited success (principally in the cases of alum and soap manufacture). Meanwhile, Commons marshaled all of its strength to fight the king's prerogative to seek rents via monopolization. After a long struggle with James over the issue, Commons revived impeachment as a means of punishing monopolists in their midst and as a means of reminding the king of their total intolerance for his claimed prerogative to seek rents in this manner. Thus, in 1621, Commons (using impeachment for the first time in almost two hundred years) denounced Sir Giles Mompesson and Sir Francis Mitchell for "fraud and oppression committed as patentees for the exclusive manufacture of gold and silver thread, for the inspection of inns and hostelries, and for the licensing of ale houses" (Taylor 1898, p. 246). The House of Lords rendered the judgment and imposed fines and imprisonment on both men. Commons' objection to the crown's supposed right to supply regulation reached its zenith in 1624, when the famous act concerning monopolies legally stripped the king of all prerogative in patents and other means to monopolize industry.[23]

In 1625 Charles I came to the throne and promptly set about attempting to restore the principle of divine right of kings, which, of course, included a reassertion of right to grant monopoly via letters patent or by order of privy council. In doing so, Charles was led to a toe-to-toe confrontation with constitutionalists, a battle he ultimately lost, along with his head, in 1649. Together with his persuasive and powerful minister Francis Bacon, who supported the royal prerogative to supply regulation, Charles found a loophole in the 1624 statute: it did not apply to "corporations for benefit of trade" or to "companies of merchants."

Thus, after the repeated refusal of Parliament to fund the king's military adventures and the king's dissolution of Parliament in 1629, Charles tried to make deals with large producers in many industries. Alum and soap monopolies had been exempted from the 1624 act, but the king encouraged the formation of huge corporations in coal, salt, brickmaking, and others, to which monopoly protection was

---

[23]Exceptions granted were for "patents of Invention" and the alum and soap monopolies. The latter were excepted because the patents were soon to expire and, further, because the privy council agreed not to renew them.

given (for fourteen years) in return for rents to the crown. Between 1629 and 1640 the alum patent brought in £126,000, with an additional revenue from soap (between 1630 and 1640) of £122,000, but the new rent seeking of Charles was doomed to failure (Nef 1968, p. 115). The circumstances of this failure should be, by now, very familiar. First, the king's monopoly protection and taxing arrangements were too costly for the merchants to continue to acquiesce to them. A competitive system in this period yielded them higher rents than could be obtained through legalized entry control, price fixing, and taxation. Thus, cartel arrangements broke down as participants blithely evaded price fixing when profitable. Second, as usual, these attempted new monopolies aroused the hostile and vociferous opposition of those merchants left out. The nonmerchant voices also joined these forces as they (correctly) perceived monopoly to be inimical to their interests (recall the wool-trade example).

Thus it was that the cartel breakdown and the more fundamental problems of enforcement brought on by the stringent objections of consumers and merchants left out combined to render the patents of Charles I ineffective three years after they were issued. Antimonopoly interests opposed to the king—reflected in self-interested inaction or adverse decisions by justices of the peace and by Commons—combined with those harboring legal and religious objections to the king's blatant and audacious assertion of supreme rights and signaled an end to his authority. In a crucial reassertion of rights, Parliament blocked, once and for all, the despotism of monarchy and established fundamental constitutional rights and the power of Parliament. Among these was the passage in 1640 of a statute putting an end to all but one of the exceptions in the statute of 1624.[24] Monarchical mercantilism was repulsed by wresting the

[24]While some of the more scientifically minded merchants and gentlemen supported the exemption of limited patents for invention in the statute of 1650 in order to encourage inventors (i.e., in permitting internalization of benefits), it is by no means the case that self-interest of members of Parliament, judges, and magistrates was not a larger factor in this decision. Nef notes, in this connection, that "the increasing industrial investments of the wealthy merchants and the improving landlords, represented in parliament, in the courts, and in the town governments, led them to welcome any invention designed to reduce costs of production and to increase profits. . . . Such industrial adventurers and their political representatives saw in the granting of patents a means of encouraging the search for the new inventions with which their prosperity was increasingly bound up" (1968, p. 119).

ability of the king to supply regulation away from him. More important for understanding the course of constitutional history and regulation, the monarch lost his ability in large part because actual and potential demanders found the effects of these regulations of very uncertain and, most often, negative benefit, given the salubrious state of the competitive system in the English economy of the time. Franchises issued by the king were not durable.

Within our analytical framework these examples demonstrate that the returns from seeking national monopoly through the state fell drastically as the conflict between Parliament and the crown intensified in the sixteenth and early seventeenth centuries. This is not to argue by any means that the conflict was motivated primarily by monopoly policy, but rather that a conflict fueled by political and religious differences had important by-products in the rent-seeking economy of England at the time. We do not assert, moreover, that the public interest, whatever this may have been in these times, played no role in the classic decisions by which the common law courts transferred monopoly-granting powers to Parliament. But the institutional realities of the centuries-old alliance between the common law courts and Parliament, together with parliamentary control over jurisdictional disputes between the two court systems, all point to the likely existence of a self-interested economic entente between common law judges and Parliament. Heckscher merely hints at these forces and offers no analysis of their effects upon the fate of national regulation. We think that they carry much importance in any balanced interpretation of the period. The remaining issue concerns the question of why Parliament was unable to operate an effective special-interest economy, that is, to effect a powerful reinstitution of mercantilist policies, after it became the sole supplier of regulatory legislation.

The Rise of Parliament and the Fall of Mercantilism

The focal point of the conflict between the crown and Parliament in the struggle to supply monopoly rights was in the area of patents. Parliament's interest lay in trying to set limits on the unlimited power of the crown to grant monopoly privileges. As we stressed in the last section, Heckscher, like most historians, tends to see the Parliament and its common-law-court allies jousting with the king over the matter of free trade. Thus:

In the latter part of Elizabeth's reign a storm broke out against her un-limited grants of patents of monopoly as rewards to her favourites and servants. The old queen, however, understood how to quiet the minds of the people with such skill that parliament refrained from making any decision on the question. The queen referred the legality of the patents of monopoly to the decisions of the ordinary courts. The patent of her courtier, Darcy, for the production and import of playing-cards gave rise to the famous Case of Monopolies (Darcy v. Allen or Allin [or Allein] 1602/3). Without any qualification and without any attempt at prevarica-tion, the decision declared the patent invalid. When James I again began to follow in Elizabeth's footsteps and grant patents, parliament once again returned to the attack. Its last and most remarkable piece of work was the Statute of Monopolies (1623/4). This memorable law introduced no essential innovations. It limited the Crown's right to granting exclu-sive patents to investors of a trade which was new to the country. For future patents the validity of the patent thus granted was not to exceed fourteen years. The final break came when Charles I once again began granting patents, and the outcome was that the regulations laid down by the Statute of Monopolies were confirmed [Heckscher 1934, 1:290].

Our interpretation of this struggle, which we feel is far more consistent with the economic environment of these times, is that both parties in the struggle sought to become the sole supplier of regula-tory legislation. We have already detailed how common law inter-pretations supported Parliament's right to grant patents as opposed to that of the crown. But there is a good deal of evidence demon-strating a direct confrontation between members of Parliament and the crown on this matter. The debate over monopolies was not a debate over free trade versus crown grants of patents, but rather over who would have the power to supply regulations. This facet of rent seeking was somewhat apparent in a *Petition of the Commons to the King, Complaining of divers Grievances*, presented to James I by the House of Commons before the closing of Parliament in 1624. Within the petition Commons claimed damage to public welfare from pat-ents granted to apothecaries, fishermen, gold wire makers, gaol-keepers, and so forth, and requested the right to grant regulation of these matters to Parliament. Of particular interest was the patent for the Wintertonness Lights. Parliament had originally issued a patent to erect and maintain the lighthouse to the master of Trinity House, who was to charge "6d. for every 20 chaldron of coals of ships passing that way." But meanwhile, one Sir John Meldrum had petitioned James for a patent to the lighthouse and had received it. The petition continues, arguing that

... though it were true, as sir John pretended, that he had petitioned to you maj. for erection of a light-house, before the said light-house of stone was erected, yet the said letters patent are void in law, for that they of the Trinity-House, having authority as is aforesaid by act of parl. did, before the said letters patent, erect a lighthouse as is aforesaid; where they of the Trinity did take but 6d. for every 20 chaldron of coals, the said sir John by colour of the said letters patent; for every 20 chaldron of coals, hath taken 3s4d. and will not suffer the ships to make their entries, or take cocquets, before they pay the said excessive duty of 3s4d. to the intolerable damage and loss of your subjects, he hath taken after the rate of 3s4d. of divers seafearing men, that sail not that way, nor in their course could take any benefit of the said light-house. Our humble Petition is, That your maj. will be pleased to publish the said letters patent to be void in law, and to command that they be no more put in execution [Corbbett 1966, p. 1492].

Though members of Parliament often cited public interest or public welfare as their rationale for wresting the patent-granting power from the crown, it is much more plausible and consistent with economic incentives that their intentions were simply to acquire the right to supply regulation themselves.

Parliament wrested these rights from the crown in numerous ways. One was, of course, to provide subsidies to the king only for a quid pro quo (which in some cases was a relinquishment of monopoly rights to the Parliament). Another was through the embarrassing exposé of blatant monarchial rent seeking. The latter occurred with increasing frequency during the reign of James I. In 1621 James's attorney general, Sir Henry Yelvington, was charged with and convicted of pocketing rents for himself and illegally attempting to restrain trade in the name of the king. Yelvington was receiving rents from a member of Parliament, Sir Giles Mompesson (who was impeached by Commons for illegal rent seeking with the crown's agent Yelvington), to enforce selectively legal complaints against hostelries licencees; of 3,000 complaints Yelvington brought 2 to trial. A more serious matter occurred in 1623–1624, when Lionel, the earl of Middlesex—the Lord Treasurer of England—was impeached by Parliament (the House of Lords) for (among other abuses) revoking existing leases on the sugar trade and issuing them to two of his own servants in exchange for bribes and under-the-table payments. James, who (to no avail) defended Middlesex, was clearly acting under the correct assumption that parliamentary impeachments pertaining to these matters would shake the royal authority to supply rent-seeking privileges, placing that power instead in the hands of Parliament (Corbbett 1966, 1:1422, 1445–1447, 1477–1478).

Heckscher offers two interpretations of these developments. He first argues that "in actual fact there is nothing which would make it probable that there was any interest on the part of the administration to systematize the industrial code in one direction or another. Nothing is more significant regarding English development after 1688 than the absence of any sign of such activity in the central government" (1934, 1:295). In this view parliamentary interests were merely dormant after seizing legislative power from the crown. Yet Heckscher develops a second interpretation, which is consistent with our argument about the predispositions of the parliamentary agents and the difficulties they faced in rehabilitating the use of regulatory legislation for revenue.

When authority was definitely transferred to parliament, this in itself meant no essential change in the political basis of industrial regulation. But it was a change in a negative direction, for it shut the door to administrative freedom of action. This result of parliamentary government may seem unlikely, since there is in England to-day what the present Lord Chief Justice, Lord Hewart, had called the "New Despotism", that is, the uncontrolled power of the bureaucracy over statutes, which has shown itself to be perfectly capable of an agreement with the constitutional pre-eminence of parliament. But there was no question of delegating the legislative authority of parliament, on which the present-day position of the English central authority is based, at a time when it had just won for itself its dominant position. Therefore the conditions for an all-embracing administrative power were not present in England in the period between the Restoration and the Parliamentary Reform of 1832. And a system of interference in all spheres of social life presupposes such a power [1934, 1:295–296].

Parliament won the competition to be the sole supplier of legislation but was unable to consolidate this power in a systematic way so as to be able to continue to garner significant revenues from grants of monopoly. Its inability to consolidate the power to pass and enforce special-interest legislation resides primarily in the higher costs of democratic relative to monarchial decision making in this respect. For example, as Heckscher emphasizes in the above quotation, there was no administrative bureaucracy in England at this time to which the task of administering economic regulation (cartel enforcement) could be delegated. Without the ability to delegate authority in this way, we know that costs of decision making in the legislature will tend to swamp the ability of legislators to monitor and control any regulatory measures they might pass (Ehrlich and Posner 1974; McCormick and Tollison 1980). Much of the evidence that Heckscher cites (1934, 1:294–325) on parliamentary attempts (failures) to seek profits through legislation ("Parliamentary Colbertism") may be interpreted in this light.

Parliamentary interests struggled long and hard with the crown for the right to operate the national system of economic regulation in England. In the end, however, when Parliament had obtained this power, it found a situation in which the costs of sustaining the bulk of the system were much larger than the (pro rata) benefits. Mercantilism thus ultimately foundered, and a significant deregulation of the internal English economy ensued. In assessing the extent of this deregulation, it should be kept in mind that Parliament was controlled by the landed class and that legislation favorable to that class was characteristic of the period. We thus characterize the deregulation of the English economy at this time as significant rather than massive. The great debate over the Corn Laws and their ultimate repeal in 1848 still lay some distance in the future.

Heckscher acknowledges this significant deregulation of the English internal economy in the post-Elizabethan period, especially after the dominance of Parliament and the common law courts was established in the post-Restoration period, after 1688 (Heckscher 1934, 1:294–297). Heckscher, however, characterizes it as an arbitrary and accidental dissolution of the old order (1:301) and attributes the decline in internal regulation solely to the inability of Parliament to delegate its authority (adherence to Locke's rule of *delegata protestas non potest delagari*). He entirely misses the point that the imposition of the *delegata* rule on Parliament simply increased the cost of supplying regulation. Policing, moreover, was very costly in this context, and it is significant that very few internal regulations actually granted in the post-Elizabethan period (such as those in the cloth industry) had to be administered by the industries themselves and enforced by the justices of the peace (Heckscher 1934, 1:296–297). Further, though Heckscher notes that legislative emphasis shifted largely (in the post-Elizabethan period) to trade restrictions and agrarian protection, he is at pains to explain the shift, changes that a public choice—regulatory perspective explain very well.

Customs, Monopoly, and Dualism

In concluding the present chapter we look briefly at the issue of tariffs and quotas, that is, at the issue of tariffs and quotas in the protection or encouragement of international competition. Clearly, the nexus of power to levy customs duties ("tonnage and poundage") shifted often from the medieval period through the seventeenth century. Indeed, one of the major factors leading to the constitutional revolt in the reign of Charles I was exactly the matter of prerogative in the matter of customs duties. Charles claimed an "ancient right" to customs, but Parliament ultimately seized, in 1641, the exclusive power to set these duties. (Parliament later gave William and Mary customs and port duty for limited terms of four years, partially as a ploy to guarantee frequent parliaments [Taylor 1898, p. 419].) While Parliament was dissolved, however, an event took place which reveals that vested rent-seeking interests were operative in the matter of trade policy. In the interim over which Charles claimed absolute authority to levy taxes, merchant importers refused (in their own interests) to pay customs to the king, obeying a remonstrance of Parliament to refuse to pay duties not authorized by Parliament. The king ordered the seizure of goods, whereupon several merchants resisted and were brought before the privy council. One of them, Richard Chambers, declared that "merchants are in no part of the world so screwed as in England. In Turkey they have more encouragement" (Taylor 1898, p. 274). Imprisonment was the cost Chambers incurred for his flippancy.

This incident, small in itself, reveals that, while motives of unification and state power building may be pressed to explain macroeconomic protectionist trade policies, self-interested rent seeking was never far from the surface in shaping those policies which we regard as typically mercantile in nature. That is to say, there is a commonality about rent seeking whether its subject is international trade controls or domestic industrial regulation. Adam Smith made this point very emphatically:

. . . in the mercantile system, the interest of the consumer is almost constantly sacrificed to that of the producer; and it seems to consider production, and not consumption, as the ultimate end and object of all industry and commerce. . . . In the restraints upon the importation of all foreign commodities which can come into competition with those of our own growth, or manufacture, the interest of the home-consumer is evidently sacrificed to that of the producer. It is altogether for the benefit of the latter, that the former is obliged to pay that enhancement of price which this monopoly almost always occasions [1937, p. 625].

While a number of writers have noted a dualism in mercantile writers' approach to domestic controls on the one hand and to protectionist mercantile policies in trade on the other, it seems that the apparent contradiction may be resolved when mercantilism is viewed as a rent-seeking activity. An example described by Heckscher will illustrate this point: "From the end of the Middle Ages onwards, the import of wool cards into England was prohibited. They constituted an important means of production in the textile industry, which normally enjoyed greater favour than any other. A decree of 1630 went so far as to proscribe the sale of cards produced within the country from worn-out patterns. The maintenance of employment was given as the official motive for the measures, but in fact, at least as regards the latter prohibition, the object was to assist one of the oldest industrial joint-stock companies, the Mineral and Battery Works" (1934, 2:148). The point that this quotation illustrates is that the official motive for protectionist measures was, in all likelihood, seldom if ever the real motive for such measures.

Most writers on mercantilism identify some sort of "homogeneous" mercantile trade policy, employment policy, population policy, domestic policy, and so on, as if interests independent of those which drive economic man in all ages were responsible for the economic policy called mercantilism. We argue that there is no reason to expect that motives that operate on the demand or supply sides of monopoly protection in domestic industries are absent when it comes to another form of monopoly-creating device. Thus, one expects to observe some division of rents between manufacturing interests and the monarch when it is observed that mercantilists sought to establish a tariff-quota system in which the export of manufactures and the import of raw materials (and vice versa) was encouraged. We agree with Smith's assessment that mercantilism is but a tissue of protectionist fallacies supported by merchants, but we go further and argue that unvarnished rent seeking by merchants, monarch, and ultimately the masses represented by Parliament explains most economic intervention, as well as a good deal of political-legal change, over the period. A philosophical dualism may have existed as philosophers were converted to individualism (Locke) and natural law as a guide to economic conduct (Mandeville, Petty, Cantillon, Hume, and Smith). But as we have seen, the philosophical revolution was fostered by the conduct of rent seekers constrained by a particular form of polity. The form of that polity, moreover, underwent fundamental change under the impetus of the interplay of these self-interested economic forces. Mercantilist writers, Jacob Viner suggests, created "an elaborate system of confused and self-contradictory argument" (1967, p. 109). Our application to mercantilism of recent theory related to economic regulation suggests that the practitioners of mercantilism were anything but confused and self-contradictory. Through their actions, self-interested individuals ultimately altered the constraints within which rent-seeking activity could take place. In fact, our conclusion significantly amplifies Viner's belief that "pleas for special interest, whether open or disguised, constituted the bulk of the mercantilist literature. The disinterested patriot or philosopher played a minor part in the development of mercantilist doctrine" (1967, p. 115).

Conclusion

In the present chapter we have argued that important institutional changes in the rent-seeking economy of mercantilist England explain the rise of free trade in these times on both internal and external levels. This interpretation is more robust than the standard interpretation of English mercantilism in that it explains both the rise and the fall of mercantilism with the same model. Thus, we have argued that the conventional mercantilist paradigm of power versus plenty offers no convenient means of explaining the decline of state interference in England. Both the conventional interpretation and our own emphasize an inherent contradiction in the mercantile system. Specifically, both interpretations emphasize wealth destruction as the main feature of the system. In the conventional interpretation wealth is dissipated in a process of specie accumulation for state power building. The process is then adjudged to have been self-defeating and irrational, owing to the quantity theory of money and its international accoutrement, the price–specie flow mechanism.

In our interpretation, on the other hand, societal wealth is dissipated through monopoly creation and rent seeking at both local and national levels. Although the process was rational and efficient from the participants' point of view, economic growth was thwarted nonetheless. A major point of the rent-seeking interpretation, however, is that the process—including the enforcement apparatus of the local regulations—unintentionally helped bring about institutional changes that made rent seeking and internal regulation by the central government less feasible. Under the altered institutional structure liberalism and free trade became viable alternatives in England. Thus, the overuse of rent extraction put in motion forces that were to limit sharply its future scope.

4

The Venal Society of Mercantile France

Monseigneur:
   The pains that you are lavishing to make commerce flourish in this kingdom have made me bold enough to offer to you this work, which I have entitled *The Complete Business Man.* I could dedicate it only to you, Monseigneur, since it is to your wise counsel that the public owes those beautiful regulations which have been made to repress disorders and to prevent misfortunes in matters of business.
                         Jacques Savary to Jean-Baptiste Colbert,
                         dedicatory preface to *Le Parfait Négociant*
                         (1675)

THE French experience at rent seeking and the environment in which it took place contrast at almost every point with England's. Many writers (as noted in chapter 1) have treated mercantilism as a monolithic set of "principles" relating to political economy and more or less uniformly applied across countries. A mere perusal of French mercantile history, however, should convince historians that the French experience was markedly different than the English. In fact, if mercantilism means "a system of extensive economic controls employed under a monarch with absolute power," one could hardly find a better example than France from the sixteenth to eighteenth centuries. As we suggested in chapter 3, we develop a separate treatment of French mercantilism, although the analytical goals are quite the same as in our treatment of English developments. In the present chapter we develop a positive-economic theory of the internal regulation of industry in mercantile France and of the effects of this regulation upon the course of French economic development and industrialization.

The most important reason for a separate treatment of the French mercantile experience is that it permits us to confront directly the explanations of economic historians for the two most important features of the French economy of the time: (1) the repressive and controlled internal economic structure and (2) the very clear emphasis (bias?) upon luxury productions at the expense of basic manufactures, a characteristic of the French economy that is often said to have impeded an industrial revolution in France. To be sure there is some divergence of explanations among historians. Though his discussion differs from ours in many important respects, Heckscher came closest to a positive-economic view of French developments. The most celebrated historical interpretation of French mercantilism, however, that of Charles Woolsey Cole (1939, 1943), falls far short of providing a satisfying explanation of these two features of the French mercantile economy. Historians are often wont to lionize certain individuals, as Carlyle did, and Cole proves no exception as he features Jean-Baptiste Colbert, Louis XIV's indomitable finance minister, as the "great man" and prime mover of the French State for the seventeenth and eighteenth centuries. Further, Cole clearly and repeatedly expresses the view that Colbert's economic reforms were in the public interest, that is, made in the interests of the French people. Nation-state building was the maximand for both the public interest and the glory of the monarch in Cole's scenario of French mercantilism.

While we do not dispute most of the details of these historical accounts of the French experience, we reject the "hero" and other major axioms of the historians and argue that positive-economic theory offers a more plausible account of these developments. We shall argue that the French political and economic environment was conducive to the self-interested supply of and demand for a massive system of economic regulation and that the success of this extensive intervention in the French economy greatly influenced French economic development up to the time of the Revolution. We shall argue further that the theory of economic regulation goes far in explaining aspects of French mercantilism that have long puzzled the historians, namely, the French mercantilists' response to innovations and their selective cartelization of industries. Thus, our interpretation is not a substitute for those of the historians, but rather it is an attempt to provide the basic organizing principles for a more satisfying analysis of the major features of the period.[1]

A very general introduction to the "venal society," wherein official positions and favors were sold by the crown, is the first order of business in the present chapter. The rise of French mercantilism, like that of English mercantilism, is explained in terms of the relative efficiency of monopoly grants over taxation as a source of revenue for the French central state. The highly effective system of enforcing the consequent monopoly and cartel arrangements is then discussed. The usefulness of analyzing French mercantilism as an example of the theory of economic regulation and efficient rent seeking is illustrated in a section dealing with the efforts of the French administrators to restrict the introduction of printed calicos in the textile industry. Rather than a mindless attack on innovations, as Heckscher and other historians would have it, we explain this episode in terms of how printed calicos altered the French administrators' costs of enforcing the mercantile economic regulations. An economic explanation of why the French mercantilists stressed luxury-oriented cartels is then offered, as is an explanation for some episodes of economic regulation that would appear to escape the analytic power of the rent-seeking approach. The latter cases refer to the basically unregulated sectors of the French economy, such as wood and iron products. We offer a positive-economic theory capable of explaining these apparent contradictions, one that contributes to our understanding of the manner in which French economic development was "warped" for the next two hundred years or so. Finally, some of the roots of the demise of French mercantilism, which lie in the treatment of rural industry and in the competition among local officials for enforcement rents, are explored. Some concluding observations are offered contrasting Cole's interpretation of French mercantilism with our own.

---

[1]Economic historians concerned with France are not, of course, a monolithic entity. We have relied upon well-known English sources, such as Cole and Heckscher, to develop our analysis. The interested reader may also wish to consult Cameron (1970) for an excellent collection of essays and sources on French economic history by French scholars. See also Nef (1968).

France as a Venal Society: The Background

The English and French experiences over the mercantile period are dramatically different. Before turning to specific issues surrounding French mercantilism, an overview of the French experience and of uniquely French institutions is warranted. Subsequently in the chapter we shall return to many of the issues raised in the following overview.

TAXATION AND VENALITY

A chief source of the differences between how the mercantile age unfolded in England and in France lies with the absolutist property rights in taxation vested in the crown from 1439 through the French Revolution of the late eighteenth century. With minor alterations the tax system of the Old Regime continued that of the Renaissance and was characterized by institutionalized venality. French monarchs shared the power to tax with the French aristocracy over the entire mercantile period. Rent seeking by the monarch in the form of contracting to enterprises or to "tax farmers" was common as early as the thirteenth and fourteenth centuries. A scholar of fiscal systems of the period aptly describes the situation: "the most important local revenues were 'farmed out' to enterprisers, who received the right to collect the domaines in return for lump sum payments. Amounts in excess of this sum became the revenue farmers' profits; and, if they collected less than the amounts paid, it was their loss—not the king's" (Wolfe 1972, p. 12. On this subject see also Hoselitz 1960.) Corruption permeated a gigantic fiscal bureaucracy, and, as in certain modern political systems, it became a way of life. Property rights shifted as the centuries passed, with tax farming and other "leases" becoming hereditary. Legal and judicial offices were sold by the crown, for example, and provide an interesting example of venality. Revealing the utter hypocrisy of the system, the oath of office in the case of justices and crown lawyers required a statement that they had not paid any money for their position. It has been observed that "for the whole sixteenth century the justices and royal lawyers began their careers with an act of perjury" (Wolfe 1972, p. 297).

Royal venality was of such magnitude, having grown throughout the period, that at the end of Louis XIII's reign (between 1636 and 1642) the French monarch was collecting between three and four times the amount of per capita taxes from his subjects as Charles I, who was then locked in a death battle with Parliament. The mercantile writer Gregory King estimated the "general income" of France in 1688 at £80,500,000 sterling and that of England at £41,700,000, estimates rough in themselves but sufficient to indicate a much larger success of royal rent seeking in France over the mercantile period (Nef 1968, p. 128).

THE INSTITUTIONAL BACKDROP OF RENT SEEKING IN FRANCE

The rent-seeking coalition of crown and aristocracy was facilitated in France by a number of institutional features stemming from and related to the absolute power to tax by the crown. There are the interrelated matters of (1) the enforcement of industrial regulation, (2) the degree of effective crown rent-seeking interference with old and new industries, and (3) the incidence of the tax structure and the incentives established thereby. After examination of each of these issues, it is clear that Heckscher's observations (1934, 1:145) regarding the design and implementation of industrial regulation in England and France is basically correct. That is, while English and French monarchs were equally zealous in establishing rent-seeking activity, the French system was far more effective at enforcement. We add to this the observation that not only was enforcement an underlying point of difference between the two systems, but an absence of other, countervailing forces in France permitted rampant venality by a royal-aristocratic coalition.

ENFORCEMENT

The guild system in France grew stronger from the time of the Middle Ages onward, in contrast to the English experience. At the opening of the sixteenth century most local industry was done by free craftsmen, but by the reign of Henry IV (1589–1610) the guild regime was dramatically strengthened. Two crown edicts (1581 and 1597) laid down uniform rules for the organization of handicrafts all over France and permitted master craftsmen who were not members of guilds to organize and obtain from royal officials all of the advantages of formal guild membership: regulated apprenticeships and entry, hours of work permitted, and so forth. Guild regulations, moreover, were confirmed by royal letters patent. The result of these activities was a massive extension of royal prerogative, superseding guild and local prerogative in the matter of decentralized royal control over industrial activity. Entry control, the imposition of maximum wage rates upon journeymen, price controls, and the establishment of rent-seeking offices engendered by all this became a centralized crown prerogative, as we shall explain later in the chapter.

Although these developments set the stage for a venal society with centralized property rights, further developments significantly strengthened the control of the king's officers over municipal authority. *Intendants des provinces*, tried servants of the crown, were sent as commissioners to the provinces to establish administrative reforms. Gradually, under the aegis of Richelieu and Louis XIII, these well-paid *intendants* took over and consolidated most of the functions of earlier royal provincial administrators, thereby permitting crown ministers far greater assurance that the crown's policies would be undertaken. Adjudication of regulatory disputes at the local level was also more and more becoming the business of the crown courts, by invocation of the principle of *cas royaux*, a principle whereby disputes over guild regulations and other industrial encumbrances could be tried in royal courts due to "crown interests." Certainly Colbert, minister of France between 1661 and 1683, must have found these inherited institutions a great advantage in implementing the intensified rent seeking of Louis XIV.

Over this important period, then, the institutions of legislative and judicial enforcement over industry and trade were developing along sharply opposing lines in England and France. During the crucial century from 1540 to 1640, institutions that facilitated rent seeking by crown and aristocracy were greatly strengthened in France, while such enforcement institutions, legal and administrative, were becoming atrophied in England. The French crown did not have to brook the combined opposition of enforcers, those disgruntled by regulation, and the public in its quest for economic rents.

INDUSTRIAL RENT SEEKING AND ECONOMIC GROWTH

The administrative machinery that served rent seekers vis-à-vis local handicraft regulation was duplicated over specific industries in a manner that could only be pitifully imitated by the English. Tight royal control over mines, saltpeter and gunpowder, and salt was greatly facilitated by decentralized local production with centralized control over rent-producing "franchises."

In the matter of saltpeter and gunpowder manufacture, the "grand master of the artillery" (the minister Sully served for a long while) was given exclusive management. In imitation of the tax-collection system, these rights were "farmed out" to commissioners who represented the grand master in granting or revoking rights to produce. Commissioners, in turn, exacted for themselves a split in the rents created.

Concession rights to the produce of mines were likewise farmed out to court favorites through an elaborate administrative machinery. Revenues in the form of lump-sum payments went to the crown, as did a regalian tax on ores (*droit du dixième*). Entry, exit, and abandonment were all regulated to the mutual advantage of aristocratic franchise holders (*concessionaires*) and the king.

The French crown, like its English counterpart, granted patents for new inventions and, along with them, money subsidies and official salaried help for inventors. But the French went further by determining the entire direction of technology. By granting a large number of limited tax-exempt concessions, kings from Henry IV and Louis XIII appear to have warped technology by shifting emphasis toward new branches of artistic craftsmanship (cloth, glass, tapestries) and away from cost-reducing devices necessary for the introduction of quantity-oriented, large-scale production. Though patents for the latter were not refused, crown advisors were establishing conditions that greatly favored the establishment of artistic productions. Such emphasis expanded into the well-known government studios and art factories of Louis XIV and his royal successors. Indeed, the details of this process—and the economic motives of the participants to it—constitute a major feature of our positive analysis of French mercantilism.

TAXES, RENT SEEKING, AND ECONOMIC GROWTH

Perhaps the single most successful application of venality by the French crown related to the salt monopoly. Claiming regalian rights (which corresponded to the salt tribute of the imperial Roman state) in most of the provinces of France, the crown imposed intricate regulations on salt producers, requiring them to sell all salt produced to royal storehouses at prices fixed by the king's officers. Consumers were then forced to purchase salt (with required quantities per parish) at rates four times as high as free-market rates. Although there were infractions, monopoly conditions were rigorously enforced, in large measure because of the effectiveness of royal representatives at the local levels.

The *gabelle* and other taxes on salt became the single most important revenue source next to the infamous *taille*. The *taille* was a tax levied on the income and real property of peasants, shopkeepers, and craftsmen who were not exempted by virtue of participation in royal manufactures. In real terms receipts from the *gabelle* rose eight or ten times between 1523 and 1641 (Nef 1968, p. 83).

The imposition of both the *gabelle* and the *taille* had stark implications for the distribution of income and economic growth. Both of these taxes and the indirect taxes on commodities fell heavily upon the poor, discouraging capital formation. Unbridled taxing powers facilitated redistributions to the nobility and to the clergy, who utilized the wealth for "artistic consumptions."

Thus, institutionalized rent seeking had a number of implications for the form of the French mercantile state. Growth in real output lagged far behind that in England because of a dearth of investment opportunities and, more importantly, a lack of incentive for capital formation. Absolutism created so much uncertainty in property rights that, as has been remarked of the Spanish mercantile system of the time, one became a student, monk, beggar, or bureaucrat since there was nothing else to be (North and Thomas 1973, p. 131). Most of the best minds, as in all societies, were attracted to the areas of highest return. In France this meant that they sought a bureaucratic sinecure, which could be passed on through hereditary rights.

The certainty of absolute power and of an imposed system of rent seeking contrasted sharply with the uncertainty of private entrepreneurial returns in France. The high private returns of a relatively unfettered competitive system, which proved sufficient to bring down mercantile monarchy in the English case, were neither extant nor possible in France. The tradition of the venal system created there was so intense and the underpinnings so strong that the emergence of a liberal order was postponed until the late eighteenth century. With these introductory observations in mind, let us now turn to a more specific and microanalytic discussion of rent seeking in mercantile France.

A Theory of French Monarchial Rent Seeking

Heckscher (1934, 1:137) sets the stage for our analysis with his observation that "from the outset, the monarchy considered it one of its chief tasks to gather to itself those powers over handicraft and trade which had fallen into other hands during the confusion of the Middle Ages." This observation is, of course, quite consistent with historians' usual emphasis on mercantilism as a system featuring the enhancement of state power relative to the combination of particularism (the natural economy) and universalism (the church) prevailing in the medieval economic order. But we would like to interpret the development of the nation-state under the mercantilists in a different way.

TAXATION VERSUS MONOPOLIZATION

The French monarchy sought revenue to finance its expenditures, and the term that we apply to this behavior is rent seeking. In a fundamental sense the situation in France was the same as we discussed for England. There were basically two sources of revenue available to the French administrators—taxation and monopoly grants. Taxation was extensive in France at this time, and, as we saw above, this aspect of revenue seeking has been covered exhaustively by historians (Wolfe 1972). The extensive use of monopoly grants to raise revenue came about during the time of Colbert, who, under pressure to raise additional revenues for the king, found monopoly grants a more efficient form of rent seeking (at the margin) than taxation. Monopoly grants at the height of Colbert's administration thus became a major source of the French state's revenues.[2] Col-

[2]Crude calculations from Cole (1939, 1:304–309) suggest that the revenue from only three monopolies (tobacco, coinage, and postage) amounted to one-half of all state revenues at roughly the midpoint of Colbert's administration (1670).

bert's shift to monopoly grants forms the basis of our interpretation of French internal economic regulation, and the change in emphasis had profound implications for the course of French economic development. For the present, however, let us review the difficulties Colbert faced with taxation and then go on to analyze the relative efficiency of monopoly grants in the revenue-seeking context of Colbert's administration.

In the medieval and early mercantile period the difficulty of taxing in all economies was related to such factors as the absence of data on transactions and the general ease of tax evasion. Moreover, as noted in chapter 3, taxation places the burden on state authorities to ascertain taxable values and to collect tax revenues. Though difficulties of tax collection and assessment and the ease of tax evasion explain the emergence of rent-seeking behavior in the early French economy, the even greater reliance on monopoly creation as a means to raise revenue in the age of Colbert (the high time of French mercantilism) admits of further explanation. In addition to the continuing general technical difficulties of collection and assessment, Colbert in 1661 faced deeply entrenched interests of a fiscal bureaucracy and a fiendishly complex tax structure.[3] Colbert's hold on the king (Louis XIV) was a function of his ability to produce revenues, so that his first order of business (when he replaced Cardinal Mazarin as Louis' finance minister) was to attempt to circumvent an encrusted tax system born of feudal and medieval traditions. At this, and in spite of his very considerable intellectual powers and machinations, he was an abject failure, as Cole clearly documents.

After several dictatorial revenue-getting measures, which alienated a massive segment of the French financial community, Colbert attempted his great reform of the tax system.[4] First, Colbert attempt-

[3]See Cole's enumeration of the nineteen major internal duties and taxes levied within and without five French provinces between 1304 and Colbert's attempted reform of 1664 (Cole 1939, 1:420–427).

[4]Institution of the Chambre de Justice by edict in 1661 permitted Colbert to try hundreds of financiers for "abuses" dating back to 1635. In this act, amounting to a legal exaction of tribute, Colbert raised over 100 million *livres*, some of which was used to buy back offices that had been sold. In addition, Colbert "revised" the *rentes*—government bonds and other obligations issued before Louis XIV's majority—by cutting the government's payment on the obligation by one-third. By decree of the Chambre or by royal edict, more than 8 million *livres* per year were saved for the state in this manner (Cole

ed "reform" of the *taille réele*, a land tax that was the single largest revenue source of the state. But there were many, many exemptions based upon privilege, bribery, and tradition, so that Colbert's use of spies, seizures, and investigations of those claiming the exemptions were to no avail. Next, because of this failure, Colbert attempted to shift the incidence of taxation, reducing the *taille*, from which so many claimed exemption, and drastically raising the *aides*, which included an internal indirect tax on commodities at the wholesale and retail levels and tolls on river and road transportation, the collection of which was farmed. But so corrupt and intimidating were the farmers of the *taille* that Colbert was again thwarted and nullified (Cole 1939, 1:305–306).

Colbert's dilemma was thus the personal urgency of retaining the king's support in the face of an inability to increase revenues sufficiently via the tax system.[5] Vested interests, coupled with the exigencies of an opulent court and the 1672 war with the Dutch, drove Colbert to "new" and "extraordinary" methods of acquiring funds (Cole 1939, 1:307–312).

Colbert thus directed his rent-seeking efforts to the granting and enforcement of monopoly rights, and the French mercantile economy took on the form of a massive web of economic regulations administered by the central state. Monopoly creation was at the margin a more reliable source of state revenue than taxation, in which the state has to bear the costs of discovering taxable values and policing corruption among tax collectors, because aspiring monopolists will reveal the present value of monopolies to the authorities in their efforts to secure such grants from the state. State officials thus do not have to seek out estimates of the value of their enforcement services in the case of monopoly grants. Rather, monopoly seekers will come

---

1939, 1:301–303). In spite of these once-and-for-all ministrations to Louis' budget, the demands were well ahead of Colbert's ability to supply funds in this manner. The attempted abolition of the hereditary features of certain offices as well as the farming of certain taxes by open bidding was also of no avail.

[5]In our opinion Cole strays wildly off the point when he concludes that Colbert's "most earnest desire was to create a [tax] system of which the keynote should be 'good order'" (1939, 1:303). Surely his "most earnest desire" was to create a lucrative sinecure for himself by providing (in any manner possible) for the greater glory and magnificence of Louis XIV.

to them, and, so long as the bidding for monopoly privileges is competitive, they will reveal to state authorities the underlying value of the monopoly rights. While these conditions did exist in England, in France they were magnified exponentially. For these underlying reasons, then, the French mercantile state found it efficient to raise revenue by creating a highly monopolized economy, and this argument is sufficient to explain the rise of the French nation-state as an extension and consolidation of monopoly power in the economy.

Our concern in the remainder of this chapter will be with showing how this rent-seeking-through-monopolization interpretation of French mercantilism can be applied to offer a more appealing explanation of the main features of French economic behavior and development over this period than that offered by the historians. This is not to argue that the historians have completely ignored the revenue-seeking aspect of French mercantilism (*fiscalisme*). There is ample evidence in Heckscher and other sources about this aspect of French mercantilism: "It illustrates the tendency of the monarchy to profit from the monopolies, and was turned into a regular institution by Henry III's great edict of 1581. . . . The state had the sole aim of continually forcing those within the industry to pay in order to exclude competition" (1934, 1:179, 183). The historians, however, have tended to treat rent seeking as a manifestation of some greater mercantile objective, such as the balance of trade, rather than making it a central element in an interpretation of the period. As we shall see, the French administrators were very ingenious and intelligent rent seekers, and interpreting their behavior as a manifestation of efficient rent seeking offers a route to a fuller understanding of the important episodes of economic regulation over the period.

THE GENESIS OF FRENCH RENT SEEKING

Rent seeking is thus our basic model, and it might be well to begin our analysis by sketching in general terms the monopolization process whereby the French nation-state consolidated its power. We begin from a situation in which monopoly power was extremely localized in the various town economies and took the form of occupational licensing arrangements and the control of access to town marketplaces. These local cartels were managed and enforced by guild officials. As in the case of England, the ostensible reason for central-state interference with the operation of the town cartels was the increase in prices and wages that followed the pestilence of the Black Death. The real aim of the monarchy, however, was a unified system of economic regulation across the country, and it took essentially two centuries to reach this goal (the famous edicts of 1581 and 1597).

Why did the monarchy intervene in the local cartel arrangements, and what explains the desire for a uniform pattern of regulation? In the early period the system of guilds and local monopolies was only weakly diffused outside Paris. In most towns a majority of the trades were not organized into monopolies (Heckscher 1934, 1:143–144). Clearly, there existed an opportunity for the monarchy to extend and enforce these local monopolies in such a way as to increase its revenues. The strengthening of the role of the French nation-state can best be explained in such simple rent-seeking terms. This interpretation makes Heckscher's repeated emphasis that the system of national regulation was fashioned on the model of the guilds much more understandable. The guild, of course, is the familiar model of economic regulation that features the usual monopoly provisions of licensed producers and restrictions on the degree of competition among license holders.

The desire for uniform national regulation in the context of the local cartels is fairly easy to understand since competition would have otherwise undermined the cartel arrangements in the towns. Uniformity in the pattern of regulated prices is thus a major aspect of the pattern of mercantile regulation in France, as it is in most systems of economic regulation. The differences that tend to appear are quite predictable in terms of a rent-seeking model. It is therefore not surprising that occupational masters who apprenticed in Paris could practice anywhere in the country they wished, while masters outside Paris did not receive the reciprocal benefit (Heckscher 1934, 1:146–147). In terms of a rent-seeking theory of government the Parisian masters were more densely populated and located closer to the source of monarchial fiat than their counterparts elsewhere in the country. They consequently faced lower organizational costs to lobby for crown protection, and they received a more inclusive monopoly as a result.[6] Other variations in regulatory uniformity appeared as a result of variation in enforcement practices, and we shall have more to say about these.

Monarchial rent seeking in France, therefore, is sufficient to explain the stress on the power of the nation-state in French mercantilism. There were rent-seeking opportunities for the central state, and economic regulation in the form of cartel expansion and enforcement ensued as a result. This rent-seeking competition took the form of a monopolist (the crown) providing cartel enforcement services, with the numerous "industries" throughout France bidding for these services. We surmise that, by presenting itself as the only agent in the process with an effective monopoly (of force), the French state was able to capture the bulk of the monopoly rents inherent in the regulation of the economy. As we shall see in the next section, these rents were not entirely "pure profits," as considerable sums had to be spent on the administration and enforcement of the economic regulations.

Enforcement of Monarchial Rent Seeking

The administrative machinery set up by the French to provide cartel-enforcement services is often admired as one of the greatest administrative accomplishments in the historical process of the development of nation-states. We view this administrative machinery as a natural expression of efficient rent seeking. That is, the enforcement system was an expression of a desire to maximize crown revenues from rent seeking.

As noted in our introduction, the primary means through which the French monarchy provided cartel enforcement services was through paid civil servants (the *intendants*).[7] The authority of the

[6]Heckscher (1934, 1:146) offers a competing hypothesis that seems generally weaker than ours: "The regulation was certainly intended to make craftsmanship more uniform throughout the country, by giving the craftsmen of more advanced districts the opportunity of propagating their skill in backward regions." See Faith and Tollison (1979) for an economic analysis of the pattern of occupational regulation in mercantile France and England.

[7]Although there is nothing analogous to an independent judiciary in mercantile France, there were the independent and powerful high courts, the *parle-*

intendants under Louis XIV and Colbert was extensive. These officers of the crown were in charge of all the other authorities in their administrative district and formed the link with the central authority in the administration of cartel enforcement. They judged many cases presented by the crown, organized and superintended tax collections, inspected and regulated industry, directed public education, and controlled the police and administration of troops and municipalities (Boulenger 1967, p. 344).

The fact that they were paid is important. As discussed in chapter 3, higher pay is a means to control malfeasance in labor contracts in which an element of "trust" is involved. This follows from, for example, the fact that the official faces a greater opportunity cost from losing his position by accepting bribes. Paid enforcement agents, then, were primarily a means to control corruption and to ensure uniform cartel enforcement across the country. Without a guarantee of honest and even enforcement, the services of the monarchy in this respect would have been worth less, and we can thus view the *intendants* as an efficient way to enforce the economic regulations of French mercantilism. This system of cartel enforcement contrasts dramatically with that of mercantile England where unpaid justices of the peace were relied upon as cartel-enforcement agents. English cartel administration was predictably lax, corrupt, uneven, and ultimately unstable, while exactly the opposite description applies to the French system of paid enforcers.

The nature of the regulations to be enforced by the *intendants* was also an expression of efficient rent-seeking policies. The monarchy not only set up uniform price-and-wage controls and restricted entry into the local cartels via the apprenticeship system, but it also sought to provide protection against competition from within the cartels. This latter condition is especially important in the enforcement of economic regulation because licensed sellers within the cartel will otherwise compete away excess profits through output expansion.

ments. In contrast to the *intendants*, positions in these courts were typically purchased and passed on within a family. We view this process as a means of rent protection, that is, individual monopolists bought these positions as a form of insurance against adverse rulings by the cartel-enforcement agents of the king. We shall have more to say about the competition between the *parlements* and the *intendants* later in the chapter.

Efficient rent seeking is thus a good working explanation for the incredibly detailed regulations governing cartel enforcement and outputs in mercantile France.

Consider the formal instructions given by Colbert and the king on August 13, 1669, to the newly appointed *commis*, or inspectors of manufactures. As cartel-enforcement provisions, they could hardly be surpassed. The inspectors were directly responsible to the *contrôleur-général* and were to secure meticulous observance of the industrial regulations laid down. The general articles of enforcement numbered sixty-five and were so detailed as to include monthly visits to workers' homes. Article 16, for example, required that "each month the wardens are to visit all the houses of workers. If the houses are located in distant villages or hamlets, the wardens may appoint sub-wardens to make the inspections and mark the goods. If the manufacture is considerable, the name of the village or hamlet is to be on the mark used by the sub-wardens" (Cole 1939, 2:420).

The general characteristics of the rules governing cartel outputs were also impressive. These regulations were incredibly detailed, on the order of a substantial planned economy, and the details were tailored to restrict the various means that cartel members could find to expand output from within the industry. Heckscher provides the following small example of the regulations.

Regulation followed the course of production. In the first place, it contained specifications regarding the handling of raw material, especially wool and the methods of dealing with it and went on to deal with all the subsequent stages of production, the most important of which were weaving and, especially, dyeing. Amongst numberless others, we will single out as an example of the weaving regulations a special *règlement* of 1718 for Burgundy and four neighbouring districts. As the *règlement* itself puts it, these districts produced woolen goods for the use of the soldiers and the general public, so that is was by no means a luxury industry. The dimensions of the cloths were specified in 18 articles for each place separately. We will confine ourselves to quoting the first five rules. The fabrics of Dijon and Selongey were to be put in reeds 1¾ ells wide, a warp was to contain 44 × 32 or 1408 threads including the selvedges, and when it came to the fulling-mill, the cloth was to be exactly one ell wide. Semur in Auxois, and Auxerre, Montbard, Avalon and Beaune were to have a warp of 43 × 32 or 1376 threads, the same width in the reed, and the same width of cloth when it left the fulling-hammer. Saulieu was to have the same width with 42 × 32 or 1340 (really 1344) threads, but it seems that the white and the more finely spun cloths were to have 74 × 32 or 2368 threads. Châtillon on the Seine and five other places were to have 1216 threads in a width of 1⅝ ells with the same variation for white cloths. The *sardis* fabric, which was produced in Bourg en Bresse and various other towns was to have only 576 threads with reeds of one ell and a width of half an ell after fulling, etc., etc. [1934, 1:160–161].

As we outlined above, the control of this system of economic regulation rested with paid agents of the monarchy, and their means of control were extensive. There was widespread inspection of production, well-regulated measurement of outputs, various marking procedures whereby outputs bore the name of the producer, town marks, and so forth. Penalties for violating the regulations consisted of the confiscation and destruction of "inferior" output, heavy fines, public mockery of the offender, and loss of one's license to practice for continued offenses. The regulations, then, formed an extensive system of output restriction. As Heckscher (1934, 1:162) observes, "No measure of control was considered too severe where it served to secure the greatest possible respect for the regulations." Indeed, Colbert instituted a system of spies in each town who were to report cartel chiselers to the local *intendant*. Another purpose of the spies appears to have been to keep an eye on the *intendants*, who, as we shall see in a later section, became less and less efficacious over the period.

The French monarchy thus devised quite efficient means to enforce economic regulation on a large scale. Paying the local enforcement agents controlled malfeasance and unevenness in the application of the regulations, problems that would have reduced the returns from monarchial rent seeking, and, moreover, the regulations governing cartel behavior appear to have provided an efficient system of output control on a massive scale.

Rent Seeking as a Useful Interpretation of French Mercantilism

Evidence for the usefulness of the rent-seeking theory as the principal explanation of internal and external economic policy is plentiful, although Heckscher and Cole ascribe such rent-seeking activity to other motives. Cole, particularly, views mercantile developments, and especially those instituted by Colbert, as initiated to provide for a strong French state and economy that would be of public benefit to the people and of glory to the sovereign (e.g., Cole 1939, 1:301, 307, 311–320, 329–330, and 2:141). Nevertheless, both Heckscher and Cole in their historical descriptions provide a great deal of evidence for the rent-seeking interpretation.

Only an idiosyncratic reading of Cole's excellent historical accounts of Colbert and French mercantile development could leave an impression of Colbert as a lawgiver or quintessential public servant. What comes through an analysis of his life and works is that he was a calculating and hard-dealing agent of the king, without fear and without pity (Cole's own description), who best served himself by serving up huge sums of money to his monarch, Louis XIV, to conduct one of the most sumptuous courts in history.[8]

THE GENERAL DIMENSIONS OF RENT SEEKING UNDER COLBERT

As evidence of Colbert's "public service," we might look briefly at some of the cartels formed during his administration. After several unsuccessful attempts, Colbert was able, in 1681, to form a tobacco monopoly that applied to the entire kingdom. The monopoly regulated all aspects of tobacco production, importation, manufacture, and sale. In spite of the heated opposition of consumers and retailers, revenues to the state multiplied rapidly—from 500,000 *livres* in 1681 and 600,000 in 1683 to an annual 30,000,000 *livres* in 1789. Colbert oversaw the conduct of the postal monopoly, which,

---

[8]The "public-spirited" Colbert, despite a relatively low birth in a family of traders, managed to acquire great wealth and massive influence for himself and for members of his family. As agent for the powerful Cardinal Mazarin, Colbert became wealthy and influential, 'receiving a growing stream of offices, benefices, and gratifications and asking for more without embarrassment" (Cole 1939, 1:283). In addition to receipt of great wealth over his career, Colbert attempted to build a family dynasty. A first cousin was made *intendant* of the army in Catalonia and of the government of Brouage; to one brother went the bishopric of Lugon; to another, the command of a company in the Navarre regiment; and to still another, the ambassadorship to England. Although Colbert's efforts to groom his son, Seignelay, as his successor did not pan out (though Seignelay did a very creditable job in control of the French navy), Colbert's philosophy is revealed with great clarity in one of his instructions to his son. Colbert admonished Seignelay that "as the chief end that he should set himself is to make himself agreeable to the king, he should work with great industry, during his whole life to know well what might be agreeable to His Majesty" (Cole 1939, 1:291).

after 1673, brought in 1,000,000 *livres* per year. United to the postal system in 1673, transport monopolies encouraged by Colbert (covering coaches and certain water transportation) brought in more than 5,500,000 *livres* per year by 1683. In 1674 Colbert forced all trades to form themselves into guilds, which then traded sums of money for statutes and regulations (Cole 1939, 1:307–309).

Cole reports that some of Colbert's intrusions met with "unhappy results." In 1674 he levied a tax in the form of a fee for the "inspection and making" of tin and pewterware. A great opposition developed, however, because such utensils were used almost exclusively by common people. Cole reports that

taken in conjunction, the stamped-paper and tinware taxes, together with the tobacco monopoly, led to resistence that at times assumed the proportions of a revolt. At Bordeaux the people of the lower classes rose, when an attempt was made to collect the tinware fee in 1675. For a time in March the city was in the hands of the mob. The people were pacified at first by concessions and promises, but it was not until November that troops could be sent there in sufficient numbers to crush the rising, by executions and the presence of soldiers. In the same year and for similar reasons, a revolt flared up in Brittany and had to be suppressed by troops, and parallel outbreaks occurred in other parts of the country [Cole 1939, 1:309].

A still more familiar rent-seeking expedient was employed by Colbert when he farmed coinage rights to a syndicate of capitalists for 630,000 *livres* in 1674. Colbert's nephew, Desmarets, and his agent, Bellinzani (in charge of managing the cartel), were bribed into silence by gifts, while the monopolists struck off 26,000,000 four-*sous* pieces, far in excess of what was permitted by contract, and reduced the fineness of coins by a twelfth. Colbert ignored the enormous profits, however, since, as Cole reports (1939, 1:310), "the syndicate assisted him in certain financial operations." Only after Colbert's death were Desmarets and Bellinzani brought to justice. One eighteenth-century wag had it that Colbert began his regime with bankruptcy and ended it by counterfeiting.

Examples of such cartelizing and monopoly-creating activity by Colbert and other French administrators could be multiplied exponentially over the mercantile period. Cole and other historians have maintained that through all of Colbert's measures ran a "keynote of economy," that Colbert "knew how hard it was to raise adequate funds, how necessary was money for the glory of the king and the strength of the state" (1939, 1:311). The modern economist has a better explanation. Aside from Colbert's own motives, which were certainly not selfless, the best explanation for the economic structure of mercantile France is that its institutions permitted rent-seeking behavior of a predictable type.

THE MATTER OF CALICOS

The superiority of a rent-seeking explanation, however, rests upon firmer support, for it allows the interpretation of historical episodes that otherwise appear to be highly irrational. The outstanding example in this regard concerns the attempt by the state to prevent the production, import, and consumption of printed calicos and other cotton goods in France.

The implications drawn by the two leading mercantile historians of this episode are noteworthy. Heckscher (1934, 1:170–175), terming the prohibitions an "attack on innovations," outlined the lengths to which cartel managers went to achieve these goals: "It is estimated that the economic measures taken in this connection cost the lives of some 16000 people, partly through executions and partly through armed affrays, without reckoning the unknown but certainly much larger number of people who were sent to the galleys, or punished in other ways. On one occasion in Valence, 77 were sentenced to be hanged, 58 were to be broken upon the wheel, 631 were sent to the galleys, one was set free and none were pardoned. But even this vigorous action did not help to attain the desired end" (1:173). Heckscher sees this episode as an irrational attempt by the administrators to stifle innovation. Cole, likewise, regards calico legislation as an "aberration of French policy" and as merely "one of a number of instances in which the French government tried to restrict or arrest the forces of technological, industrial or commercial change" (Cole 1943, p. 177).

The French textile industry (silk, linen, and wool productions) was the object of intense cartelization long before the time of Colbert, although Colbert cartelized these areas with renewed vigor (Cole 1939, pp. 132–237). Private traders and the East India Company, which was created by Colbert in 1663–1664 (See 1927, pp. 157–174), were responsible for the import of printed calicos into

France. No attempt was made by Colbert (who died in 1683) or by his successor Seignelay (not Colbert's son, but 39-percent owner and president of the East India Company) to bring calicos under the umbrella of regulation. Before 1681, moreover, the Huguenots, already relegated to the role of second-class citizens, manufactured, within guilds, imitation calicos, which were consumed largely by the poor.

In 1681 a boom occurred in calico demand, causing guild leaders of the wool, cloth, silk, and linen industries to complain to local *intendants* of unfair competition and unemployment within their ranks. The response, in spite of Seignelay's personal interests, was a ban in 1686 on both the domestic production and the import of calicos—a ban that may have adversely affected the cotton industry in France until the late nineteenth century. After the absolute ban in 1686 a number of "deals" took place whereby the king earned rents and the East India Company was permitted exclusive but very limited importation rights. Regulation of varying degrees of exclusiveness and severity took place between 1686 and 1700, with an absolute ban between 1700 and 1753, although a good deal of smuggling undoubtedly took place over the entire period, since the demand for calicos was strong and growing (Cole 1943, pp. 164–177).

The question that economic historians have been at pains to answer concerning this episode concerns the extent of the enforcement and policing of the ban against printed calicos. Punishment was extreme, though perhaps less extreme than described by Heckscher.[9]

[9]Punishment was inconsistent, possibly because some local *intendants* were bribed. Though punishment was meted out in varying degrees of severity to offending merchants, printers, and smugglers, there are good reasons to doubt Heckscher's estimate that 16,000 people were put to death. Unfortunately, Heckscher is as vague as to the time period he is considering as he is to what constitutes a calico-related death. Huguenot persecution in France between 1680 and 1720, according to one authority (Scoville 1960), resulted in only 200 deaths related to the production of calicos. The underlying cause of Huguenot persecution appears to have been the desire to rid France of Calvinists (the Edict of Nantes was repealed in 1684). Cole (1943, p. 173) argues that most sanctions from 1686 to 1759 were monetary, though he does note that there were occasional executions in port cities. Cotton riots occured in Rouen in 1752, but only fifteen people were killed (Rudé 1964, p. 22). Thus, other sources do not tend to corroborate Heckscher's estimate of 16,000 deaths. Even several thousand killed over the matter of calicos is significant, however.

Enforcement was extended after 1700 to a prohibition against the wearing of calicos in France.[10] But was this policy the result of irrational motives or a mindless attack on innovations, as Cole and Heckscher have argued?

These arguments simply fall short by failing to consider the implications of the calicos for the managers of French economic regulation. Two basic points are relevant in this regard. As noted above, the cartel managers had to contend with the reaction of the producers of substitute textile products (the wool, cloth, silk, and linen producers). Calico production would have encroached upon these markets, and it is no mystery why these producers would have sought to ban the production of calicos.

The reaction of the producers of competing goods, however, does not explain why calicos were banned. Given the rents inherent in regulating the production of calicos, it seems reasonable to expect that the French administrators would have found a way to capture these rents and at the same time mollify the producers of substitutes (side payments?). The answer to this part of the puzzle lies in the fact that the management of economic regulation is less costly when the industry produces a homogeneous product. The price, entry, and output controls of French mercantilism could be more effectively implemented where cloth of uniform colors and sizes was produced. Indeed, uniformity was carried to the extreme in the previously described incredibly detailed regulation of the French textile industry (Cole 1939, 2:156–158 and 1943, p. 48).[11] The printed calicos thus presented a threat of no small importance to the French tex-

[10]Spies of the government, in the words of Cole, were soon "peering into coaches and private houses and reporting that the governess of the marquis de Cormoy had been 'seen at her window clothed in calico of a white background with big red flowers, almost new or that the wife of a lemonade-seller had been seen in her shop in a casaquin of calico,' " (1943, p. 176).

[11]In March, 1671, Colbert had a "general Instruction for the dyeing of wool and manufactures of wool in all colors . . ." prepared and published. The Instructions contained 317 articles and were incredibly detailed: "Those [fabrics] that are to be dyed black should be boiled with gall and sumach, and, lacking sumach, with myrtle-leaved sumach [*Rhus myrtifolis*] of *fovic* [a native French plant]; being well galled, they have a color between fallow and gray; and it will be observed that fallow and root color are really the same thing" (example in Cole 1939, 2:408). Instructions such as these are added evidence of an extreme attempt to control quality competition within the textile cartels.

tile cartel—product differentiation. These colored cloths raised costs to the regulatory managers, because product differentiation opened the door to nonprice competition. Even where the cartel price was controlled and where there were extensive controls on entry from without and within, the introduction of the printed calicos would have meant that licensed calico firms could have competed for expanded market shares through quality (pattern and color) competition. Such nonprice competition would have dissipated excess profits within the cartel, an outcome that was in the interests of neither the regulatory managers nor the regulated firms (Stigler 1968; Douglas and Miller 1974).

When taken with the religious controversy, then, these two basic reasons—the reaction of producers of substitutes and the difficulty of regulating nonprice competition—show the response of the French mercantilists to calicos to be a highly rational expression of efficient rent seeking and not a mindless attack on innovation. Numerous other examples may be drawn from Cole, Heckscher, and various other sources to illustrate the usefulness of the rent-seeking theory in interpreting French internal regulation.[12] The example of printed calicos is sufficiently dramatic, however, to illustrate the usefulness of the theory.

[12]Heckscher's example of button-making speaks for itself: "Button-making was controlled by various organizations, according to the particular materials that were used, although the most important part of the business belonged to the cord- and button-makers' gild. And so, when tailors and dealers began to produce buttons from the same material as the particular cloth used and even to use woven instead of hand-made buttons, the button-makers raised terrific opposition. The government came to their aid, in the first place because they considered the innovation an outrage against a settled industry of good standing, and secondly, because it adversely affected handicraft (1694–1700). A fine was imposed not only on the production and sale of the new sort of buttons, but also on those who wore them, and the fine was continually increased. The wardens even demanded the right to be allowed to search people's houses and claimed police aid to be able to arrest anybody in the street who wore unlawful buttons. When the otherwise extremely zealous and conscientious chief of the Paris police, de la Reynie, would have denied them this, he received a severe reproof and even had to apologize" (1934, 1:171–172). Cole (1943, pp. 177–179) describes some of the difficulties of enforcement. *Intendants* in the provinces complained that the buttonmakers themselves were willing to make illegal buttons at the tailor's request. In 1698 an *intendant* from Provence complained that he could not enforce the law since

Luxury-Oriented Cartels and French Economic Development

One of the most perplexing problems associated with French mercantile history is related to the very apparent encouragement of luxury industries through protective cartels and the clear neglect of certain basic industries such as iron and wood products.[13] (By neglect we simply mean a failure to cartelize, protect, and encourage.) This feature of French mercantile policy has figured prominently in historians' stock-in-trade explanation of the tardiness of industrialization in France. As one historian of the period put it: "Although the French boasted that their country was nearly self-sufficient because of its abundant natural riches, their governments . . . showed much more interest in expanding manufacturing and trade than in exploiting the land and its produce" (Mettam 1977, p. 230). Still another example is the French economic policy toward iron production. The managers of economic regulation offered no cartel services for this industry. Heckscher describes the situation: "There is no lack of contemporary statements to the effect that the usual type of French economic policy tended to obstruct the development of iron production. For instance, the head of an iron works wrote, 'Glass manufacturers, manufacturers of genuine porcelain and faience, cloth manufactures, embroidery concerns, silk and gold-lace production, all enjoy every possible privilege and exemption; iron manufacturers alone have no advantages, and yet they cater for real needs while the others serve only luxury and comfort' " (1934, 1: 198–199).

The important question, then, is why the French administrators sought rents primarily by cartelizing luxury industries. The traditional answers, which we will analyze, are distinctly unsatisfying, and we believe that positive-economic analysis offers a far better explanation.

---

news had come to the "people of quality" in his province that illegal buttons were being worn openly at Paris and Versailles.

[13]In his doctrinal survey of French mercantile thought before Colbert, Cole traces the strands of early antiluxury sentiment in France primarily to the ethic of Christian humility (1931, pp. 215–216). These views gave way, however, to the "spirit of bullionism" and, chiefly, to the recognition of the profitability of state-enfranchised luxury cartels, so that from the time of Colbert France has supplied a large part of the world with luxury goods.

TRADITIONAL EXPLANATIONS

Consider two traditional explanations. First, there is the luxury-consumption argument. In this case the French monarch and aristocracy are seen as the major demanders of luxury goods. They therefore had a direct interest in regulating the quality of their purchases. As examples, one could look at the tobacco monopoly already considered and at tapestry manufacture, the latter a good example of a totally state-directed cartel (Cole 1939, 2:287). This argument, though, ignores the facts that basic materials must also have been demanded by aristocrats (certainly indirectly as luxury items) and that cartel managers could have earned rents by cartelizing any industry, basic or otherwise.

A second line of reasoning, congruent with the luxury-consumption argument, is that import substitution should be prevented for luxury productions. Indeed, most of the goods imported to France were luxury goods. As Cole describes the situation: "Royal letters of 1554, confirming the statutes of the workers in cloth of gold, cloth of silver, and silk in the city of Lyon, spoke of the establishment of such manufactures as the only way to prevent the export of money. In 1572 an edict evinced a desire on the part of the king that the French devote themselves to the manufacture and working up of wool, flax, hemp, and tow, which are produced abundantly in this kingdom . . . and from them make and get the profit that the foreigners (now) make, who come to buy them generally at a low price, export them, have them worked up, and then bring back the woolens and linens to sell at high prices" (1939, 1:9).

In this argument luxury cartels were formed to "expropriate" rents from foreigners. The lace industry provides a clear example of protectionist cant ("protect domestic employment") to support baser motives.[14] Certainly this could have been one of the reasons—

[14]In May, 1665, a royal proclamation was issued establishing monopoly privileges for the manufacture of lace in order to prevent "the export of money and to give employment to the people" (Cole 1939, 2:239). In return for rents from lace manufacturers, the state enforced the cartel by precluding anyone other than the franchisees from making lace. In order to discourage smuggling and cheating, more edicts were required—the wearing of foreign lace was prohibited after 1667. More importantly, fixed places of manufacture had to be established. As Colbert wrote to a lace supervisor: "I beg you to note with care that no girl must be allowed to work at the home of her

especially when combined with the luxury-demand argument—for
the establishment of luxury-directed cartels. It would give substance,
moreover, to the so-called mercantile policy of importing raw materials and exporting finished goods, the "balance-of-labor" axiom of
mercantilism. However, this latter argument ignores the fact that
much, and in some cases (for example, tapestries) all, of the output
of French luxury manufactures was consumed within France and not
manufactured for export. However, it is not clear on the basis of the
import-substitution argument why the directors of French mercantilism would not have wanted to be independent in all productions or
why rents could not have been earned by cartelizing raw-materials
production or other inputs, such as steel.

RENT-SEEKING EXPLANATIONS

The rent-seeking model provides the basis of a good explanation
of this important aspect of French mercantilism, and three points are
fundamental in this respect. First, certain basic production was not
cartelized because the government itself was a major direct demand-
er of industry output. For example, we find some interesting instructions regarding the supply of wood to the navy in a letter from Colbert to an official:

> The purchase of forests to be managed at the expense and under the
> care of His Majesty could never be advantageous, and there are grounds
> for astonishment that you should make such a proposition, which is sub-
> ject to so many inconveniences which are so easy to see that it should not
> even be thought of.
> If there are forests for sale in Provence and Dauphine you must stimu-
> late the merchants to purchase them, and make bargains with them to
> supply all sorts of wood to the navy at the best price possible [Cole 1939,
> 1:350].

The government thus did not offer cartel services to certain basic
industries—especially those involved in the production of public
goods—but rather acted as a *monopsonist* in these cases, buying
lumber and other basic inputs at the best terms available.[15]

---

parents and that you must oblige them all to go to the house of the manufactures. . . ." (Cole 1939, 2:248).

[15]Monopsony buying from competitively organized suppliers of military
equipment seems to have been an entrenched practice under Colbert. Vast
quantities of munitions, and especially small arms (pikes, muskets, pistols,

Other rent-seeking schemes for the supply of public goods were used in France from medieval times. Competitive bidding by private entrepreneurs for the right to supply armaments, fortifications, canals, and so forth, was a distinct feature of the French fiscal super-structure (Hoselitz 1960; Ekelund and Hébert, forthcoming). Demsetz (1968) discusses a modern form of this system. In a rent-seeking context, however, we would not normally expect government to be concerned about efficiency in the production of publicly provided services by following, for example, the dictates of the Demsetz model. Nonetheless, in the case of the French mercantilists the state was a major buyer of certain commodities, and it therefore sought to capture rents in these situations through monopsonistic behavior. Iron and other basic inputs were consequently left unregulated. Moreover, to the extent that this monopsonistic behavior extracted rents from producers of basic commodities that would otherwise have been used for expansion or innovation, a linkage can be established between the rent-seeking theory and the retardation of French industrial growth.

A second reason for luxury-oriented cartels is that raw materials and basic industrial suppliers, located mainly in the countryside, were competitive suppliers of inputs to the cartelized luxury industries located in cities and towns. The crown was receiving regulatory rents from the latter industries, and in principle the crown's receipts would have been the same, regardless of whether the cartel tax was levied at the raw-material or finished-good stage of production. In other words, to cartelize basic suppliers and then force cartelized luxury-goods producers to pay cartel prices for inputs would have been redundant. Regulatory profits would have been the same had monopoly existed at any point in the production chain (Stigler 1951).

Consider the following example. Figure 2 illustrates the demand and cost functions for some luxury good, let us say fine furniture. Assume that both wood and furniture producers are constant-cost industries and that MC_F represents all the costs of producing furniture except lumber costs. Clearly, if both industries were competitively organized, assuming fixed proportions between inputs and out-

---

swords, and so on), were purchased by the French army and navy in this fashion (see Cole 1939, 2:340, for example). Colbert also "fostered" the competitively organized iron industry in this manner (Cole 1939, 2:328–329).

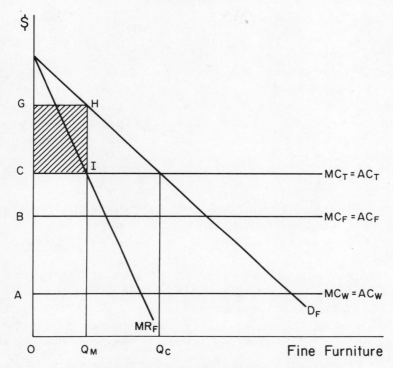

FIGURE 2. Demand and Cost Functions for Fine Furniture

puts, the price and quantity of furniture would be OC and Q_C, a price representing the vertical addition of all furniture costs and a quantity determined at the intersection of average costs and the demand (average revenue) curve.

If furniture manufacturers were cartelized, they would face a competitive input price for wood of OA (per unit) and could produce Q_C at a selling price of OC. The cartel, however, acting as a single monopolist, will reduce the output of fine furniture—in the limit to Q_M at price OG. In this manner furniture cartel managers extract $CGHI$ in monopoly rents from consumers of fine furniture.

Consider the situation, however, if fine furniture manufacturers are competitively organized, but the wood input suppliers are organized into a cartel. (As a simplification, wood products are assumed to be used only for fine furniture.) How much would a producers' cartel now charge furniture makers? With full information wood producers would know that the monopoly rate on the final output of fine furniture was OG (per unit). They (the wood producers) would thus restrict the output of wood and charge furniture makers a rate OG, the monopoly price of fine furniture, minus OB, the average cost of producing furniture (less wood costs). The resulting per-unit rate for wood (BG in figure 2), when added to the furniture producers' costs (less OB, the cost of lumber), produces an average cost to the competitive furniture makers of OG per unit. A quantity, Q_M, of furniture is produced and sold at the "retail" level; furniture producers earn only "normal" competitive returns; and wood producers exact a cartel-monopoly rent (ultimately from consumers of the final product) of $CGHI$. To the French cartel manager, then, it would have made no difference in terms of regulatory profits where the cartel was located, assuming only that organization, policing, and enforcement costs were identical. This brings us to a third crucial point.

In general, a profitable cartel requires successful enforcement and policing so that competition does not erode profits. But in mercantile France, nonluxury industries tended to be located away from towns, presenting the problem of rural regulatory enforcement. Rural economic regulation was difficult because the opportunities to cheat on cartel arrangements in a vast rural sector were numerous. By contrast regulation of a luxury industry agglomerated in cities was far less costly to the regulatory authorities. Organizational and enforcement costs influenced which industries would be cartelized since basic-industry and raw-materials production were simply too costly to organize in this fashion.

Thus, monopsony, efficient rent seeking, and enforcement costs explain the so-called bias toward luxury cartels. Such a regulatory scheme was rational and readily understandable, given the economic incentives facing the French regulatory managers. It seems undeniable that such a pattern of rent seeking would dramatically affect the pattern and pace of French economic development. While we do not wish to become directly involved here in the heated discussion over whether French economic growth "stagnated" over the period or whether France ever went through an Industrial Revolution (see Roehl's [1976] proposed resolution of the matter, for instance), certain features of our cartel interpretation may be very relevant to this question. It seems clear, for instance, that the unwillingness to tamper with profitable cartels retarded the introduction of certain kinds of technology, but that, once they were introduced, the government tended to capture the rewards from innovation. Looms, for example, were invented early in the seventeenth century, but they were principally used for producing silk stockings. When the technology began to be applied to the manufacture of woolen and linen goods, the reaction of the handknitters (an industry Colbert was fostering at the time) was entirely predictable. By decree in 1680 Colbert outlawed the use of looms on any article except silk. But the users of the new technology were powerful enough to pressure the government in 1684 to give them their own protective legislation, contravening the order of 1680. All sorts of offensive and defensive restrictions followed, with the government trying to take rents from both sides (Cole 1943, pp. 177–179). Such activities within cartels must have taken a toll on the profitability of new technology, reducing the rewards for invention and innovation, with predictable effects upon economic growth. Still other kinds of cartels that must have suppressed creativity were Colbert's monopoly creations in the fine arts and academics, for example, in the teaching of arts and sciences (Cole 1939, 1:314–319). Doubtless, then, the cartel theory plays an important role in explaining French economic growth over this period, but a great deal more work is needed to assess this role quantitatively.

The Devolution of Mercantile Regulations in France

An exact date for the disappearance of mercantilism from France is very elusive, as it is in the case of England or any other mercantile country. Mercantile laws or edicts may be regarded as historical facts, whereas mercantilism as an operative system under which people live is dependent upon whether these laws are enforced or not. Mercantile laws, for instance, remained on the books in England long after they were enforced or enforceable—some remain still. In the present section we seek to present some arguments for the decline of centrally directed, monarchial mercantilism in France up to the Revolution of 1789. We do not attempt to date an absolute end of mercantilism in France, since it may be perfectly reasonable to argue that only the form of rent seeking changed under

Napoleon after the Revolution. However, we do argue that two major institutional features of the French economic and political structure give us some insights into how the decline of traditional mercantilism took place. The first, which we discussed briefly in the previous section, deals with an emerging free-trade zone in the countryside, and the second concerns the competition between crown interests and local judicial interests for enforcement rents.

THE COUNTRYSIDE AS A FREE-TRADE ZONE

Rural industry was a thorn in the side of the French regulatory managers, as it was in the comparable English case. This resulted primarily from the fact that it was not economically efficient for the administrators to attempt to effect a detailed control of rural production. Several aspects of this problem are of interest for the long-run fate of French mercantilism, however.

The orginal intent of the regulatory managers was quite clearly to cartelize the whole country on the model of the guilds. Heckscher puts the matter as follows:

> The most vital step was the great *règlements* of the time of Colbert. In principle, Colbert followed the line of policy formerly adhered to by the monarchy, in applying the industrial statutes over the whole country. This provision was intended to apply to the *règlements*, to which in theory there were to be no local or other exceptions. For rural industry this signified a theoretical right to exist. The *règlements* assisted the regulation of handicrafts outside the ambit of city politics. To this extent mercantilism took its programme seriously of creating unity within the state as a whole and thus paved the way for new social forces. On the other hand, the system of regulation brought into being rules for the practice of crafts which, while going into every detail of technical production, tried to fit it into a system created by the gilds and adapted to high-grade products. And this was particularly unwelcome to the rural industry of the old type, untrammelled as it was by regulations, arising here and there to cater for the needs of producers and consumers and confined in the main to coarse and simple brands, of which the latter, which counteracted rural industry, was undoubtedly the more important [1934, 1:206].

As Heckscher senses here, the results of most legislation (or decrees) diverge considerably from the stated objectives. This is standard fare in the implementation of political programs. So it should come as no surprise that the regulatory managers in mercantile France ultimately found it uneconomic to extend the guild model to the countryside. As Heckscher observes: "It may safely be said that not only did the attempt to create gilds in rural areas fail almost completely, but the inefficiency of the innumerable regulations diminished in proportion to the distance from towns which had gild organization. There is a sufficiency of official data to confirm this, especially in the 18th century. The rural population obstinately opposed all state encroachment, even to the extent of offering personal violence to agents of the administration" (1934, 1:210).

Other forces besides enforcement costs also pushed for lax enforcement of the regulations in the countryside. Perhaps the most important additional pressure came from certain municipal entrepreneurs who wanted to be able to procure the benefits of lower-cost, rural labor. Consider Heckscher (1934, 1:211) on this point: "This was partly due to the already mentioned antagonism between the municipal entrepreneurs and their workers inside the cities, because the state sided with the entrepreneurs in their endeavours to exploit the less 'class-conscious' rural population with its lower wage standards."

What we have, as a result of rising marginal costs of extending and enforcing the system of regulation and as a result of pressures from municipal entrepreneurs, is a more or less de facto free-trade zone in the French countryside. As in the English case, this unregulated sector checked the power of the monarchial cartel and created generalized pressures toward competition. However, the rural free-trade area did not have the same significant effect that it did in England. A possible explanation of this difference is that the French government's greater but not complete police control was able to prevent large-scale but not small-scale developments in rural areas. For example, it was easier to police the production of luxuries, which of necessity had to be sold to a limited number of people and hence had to be retailed in places where they congregated. In general, however, we would agree with Heckscher, who concludes that "the French government did seek to apply the general rules to rural areas but they always had to yield to the impossibility of enforcing them" (1934, 1:212).

PARLEMENTS AND THE DECLINE OF MONARCHIAL MERCANTILISM

We have argued that the form of internal French mercantilism was well structured—it was essentially the cartelization and rent expropriation of industry based upon the guild model of restrictions. But we have oversimplified the process somewhat by failing to note that the power to rent seek at the provincial and local levels was, over the entire mercantile period, the object of competition between two opposing factions, the judiciary or *parlements* in cities and provinces and the crown and its agents—ministers, *contrôleurs*, and *intendants*. (Though the judicial system of France was more complex over the period, we adopt the term *parlements* as a simplification.) Our point is that competition for local administrative control of the cartel-enforcement process and other rent-seeking activities led to situations wherein rent seeking was less feasible. Moreover, this competition for rent-seeking power may have been an additional factor precipitating the French Revolution.

First, let us look briefly at the development of the *parlements* prior to and during the high time of French mercantilism. The *parlement* of Paris was organized in 1302, with most others having been formed by mid-sixteenth century (Lough 1960, p. 119). They were originally established as sovereign courts of the provinces subservient only to the king, and it was through their legal authority that the monarch was able to tame the feudal aristocracy and to interpose sovereign power at the local level (Lough 1960, p. 128; Lefebvre 1947, p. 17). All local taxes after 1401, for example, required the approval of the king (Lewis 1968, p. 260). Judicial *parlements*, therefore, filled the lacuna left by the decline of monarchical subjugation of the feudal aristocracy.

As we have said, French mercantile policy was a massive attempt to cartelize industry along the lines of the guild system. Although we have treated rents from this system monolithically, they were actually of two different kinds: *sanction rents*, arising from the actual recognition, licensing, or franchising of cartels, and *enforcement rents*, those emerging from the day-to-day enforcement of the cartels at the local level. Sanction rents automatically went to the monarch, while enforcement rents could potentially be captured by local enforcement officials, for example, by the *intendants* and the officials of the *parlements*.

In the early French mercantile period the chief enforcers of crown regulations were the sovereign courts, but a number of features made them poor intermediaries in the receipt of enforcement rents for the crown. Boulenger (1967, p. 90) reports that the "independent nature" of judges, the hereditary (and blatantly venalized) judgeships, and the fact that pay came from local sources all combined to produce reduced levels of rents flowing to the monarch.

The crown therefore established a more reliable method of enforcement in the form of well-paid *intendants*, a system which reached its apogee under Louis XIV. Their efficiency has already been made evident. It is important to note, however, that *intendancies* were originally temporary, covering indeterminant territories, but that later under Colbert the officials became permanently ensconced, with specific geographic areas under their control. Indeed, Colbert's dream of enlarged powers for the central government involved a radical relocation of legal authority: "Colbert sought ever to strengthen the central government and to create unity and order. The power of the governors and of the Assembly of the Clergy was reduced. By firmness and by a judicious distribution of favors, the ancient prerogatives of the *parlements* were limited, and Colbert was delighted to see the humiliation of the legal folk for whom he had an intense dislike. In similar fashion the rights of the municipalities and of the provincial estates were gradually circumscribed. On the other hand the powers and influence of the intendants, and other bourgeois officials dependent directly on the king, were gradually strengthened" (Cole 1939, 1:313). Thus, the *intendants* were originally used to strip power from provincial, local, and *parlement* administrations, and under Louis XIV their powers were effective and vast. But gradually these enforcers became poorer rent collectors for the king and far better collectors for themselves.

During the *intendants'* "introductory" period, after Louis XII, the *parlements* reacted with great hostility to their incursions. Some of their demands were that the *intendants* be abolished, that no new offices be created, that they have approval power over new taxes, and that a law of habeas corpus be enacted (Chambers 1974, 2:

551). These demands, ignored at the time, very clearly did not represent a selfless opposition to absolutism and monarchy. Rather, they represented a means through which local enforcement rents could be captured by local officials themselves.

The *parlements'* fundamental political power was that of registering and remonstrating against the king's edicts, since edicts had no force of law until registered by *parlement*. This "veto power" was not absolute but was at times effective, though under Louis XIV these rights were abrogated, only to be reinstated after his death. (These powers were very influential in the ultimate destruction of French absolutism).

The *parlements'* (ultimately successful) opposition to the crown was not the product of an attempt to support "the medieval aspects of the system," as Heckscher argued (1934, 1:156), but rather it was the inevitable result of the crown's expropriation of the *parlements'* enforcement rents.[16] During the eighteenth century, the *parlements* struggled with the crown for the privileges of the nobility and for "the exercise of political power in its interest" (Lough 1960, p. 129), and later in the century the *parlements* pushed for a return of the control of local administration. The attempt to have local powers restored simply reflects a desire to recoup enforcement rents, which, by the 1770's and 1780's, were being captured by the permanently entrenched *intendants*, who had lately become part of the "nobility" (Lefebvre 1947, p. 17).

We conclude that the conflicts engendered between crown and *parlements* over the power to seek enforcement rents had a great impact upon the decline of the monarchy and upon the manner of the Ancient Regime's end. Monarchial mercantilism in France declined contemporaneously with this struggle, but the struggle was not over the legitimacy of cartel formation or rent seeking. It was simply

[16]Other examples of the *parlements'* acting in their own self-interest could be given. The *parlement* attacked the crown during the Fronde because it "would deprive 'officers' of many of their powers, and thus in the long run reduce the value of their posts" (Lough 1969, p. 129). The crown faced its greatest opposition when it tried to increase the number of *parlementaires* (Moote 1971, p. 53) and when it tried to "carry out a proper land survey" (Lough 1960, p. 182) in order to make a more just levying of the land tax, a policy which would have required the *parlementaires* to pay more tax.

a contest over the locus of the rent-seeking power and in this respect is very analogous to the decline of English mercantilism.

Conclusion

We shall have more to say about the parallels and contrasts between English and French mercantilism in our concluding chapter. For now, we would like to compare our approach to French mercantilism with that of Cole, who along with Heckscher is the major prevailing scholar of French developments.

Cole presents a very misleading epitaph on French mercantilism when he notes that, since French mercantilism "was organized and administered by an officialdom which sought and aimed to serve the interests of the nation as a whole, under a monarch who was definitely not desirous of serving the bourgeois class more than others, it is probably incorrect to think of mercantilism in France as a class instrument or to attempt to interpret it as part of a class struggle, or to hold, even, that it sprang exclusively from the needs of the bourgeoisie, as a class" (1939, 2:554).

Cole thus attempts to counter the Marxian view of mercantilism as a class struggle by claiming that national unity was the basic aim of mercantile policies. But we argue that Cole is correct for the wrong reasons. The Marxist argument is very weak exactly because of the neutral nature of the struggle to acquire the regulatory apparatus: "Capital" does not use the State to exploit "Labor." As we have seen, labor may be just as likely to use the regulatory apparatus to further its own interests (for example, in the Statute of Artificers) at the expense of other interests. At times, one group captures the apparatus; at other times, another. Thus, the rent-seeking theory of economic regulation is not a Marxian theory, but, rather, it permits an explanation of why and when certain interests tend to dominate the mercantile landscape.

Cole, moreover, in his protracted quest to characterize mercantilism as a coherent group of policies, theories, and practices, presents a basically "supply-driven" definition of French mercantilism. "Mercantilism in France means that group of theories, policies, and practices arising from the traditions of the country and the conditions of the time, and upheld and applied by Jean-Baptiste Colbert during his years in office, 1661–83, in his efforts to secure for the nation, and for the king who symbolized it, power, wealth, and prosperity" (Cole 1939, 2:558, sentence in italics in original). In contrasting English and French mercantilism, Cole further serves up the following figure of speech: "the English business interests were a batch of squalling children crying for candy and getting it from a somewhat inattentive mother, Parliament. The French business interests, less vocal though no less childlike, were made to behave in a manner which a more attentive mother—the royal government—believed to be for the best interests of all concerned" (1939, 2:533). We simply wish to emphasize that regulation, policies, and practices in both countries over the mercantile age were driven by very adult supply and demand forces. There is small evidence, further, for interpreting Colbert's massive supply of regulation as oriented to the public interest. Colbert was simply a superb rent seeker for the king and for himself. And moreover, there is a great deal of evidence—much of it provided by Cole himself—that rents were shared with business interests, which demanded and acquired cartel privileges.

5

Industrial Organization in the Mercantile Age

A part of that force which always intends evil always creates good.

Goethe, *Faust*

A positive-economic theory of mercantilism has been developed in this book—one that completes the historical record with an explanation of the course of state intervention in the English and French mercantile economies. Our explanation is couched in terms of modern contributions to the theory of economic regulation and is based upon the costs and benefits facing individual economic agents in the mercantilist historical context as they sought to use the power of the state to increase their wealth.

This analysis is extended in the present chapter to consider the regulation of mercantilist foreign trade. Our particular interest in analyzing the regulation of international trade in these early economies is in developing a plausible linkage between the various forms that this regulation took and the types of business organizations that emerged to engage in foreign trade. By no means the only, but perhaps the most interesting, aspect of our analysis will be the development of a new and more complete hypothesis about the origin of that early forerunner of the modern corporation, the English joint-stock company.

We begin with a simple cartel theory of the early English foreign-trading firms (the "regulated companies"), in which various manifestations of cartel arrangements are discussed. Next we analyze the comparative economic performance of the trading companies in the various mercantile economies, which is viewed as a manifestation of the differing institutional environments within which the companies operated. The Dutch companies' efficiency, for example, re-sulted from the difficulties of suppressing competition among the Dutch towns, while the Portuguese, Spanish, and French companies exhibited the predictable inefficiency resulting from public control and operation of enterprise.

An expanded hypothesis about why the joint-stock form of eco-nomic organization emerged from the English regulated companies is then presented. The traditional hypothesis about the legal invention of the corporation, contained in Heckscher and various other sources, is based on a demand-for-capital argument. Contractual provisions, such as limited liability, and economic features, such as risk pooling, are seen as enhancing the ability of the early trading companies to raise capital in the demand-for-capital hypothesis. These companies presumably required an expanded capital base in order to develop a more elaborate infrastructure (for example, fortifications) for their foreign-trading operations. Our hypothesis expands this argu-ment to consider the English joint-stock companies as a legal device enhancing the transferability of shares in the foreign-trading cartels. With the advent of the joint-stock form, for example, cartel shares did not have to be passed on in the family (as in the regulated companies), but could be capitalized and sold to those who had a comparative advantage in cartel ownership and management. Thus, an important source of inspiration for the emergence of the cor-porate form came from the supply side and was based on the desire of cartel owner-managers to operate their foreign-trading monopolies more efficiently. A related issue from the history of economic thought, namely Adam Smith's well-known views on the inefficiency and limitations of the joint-stock form of business organization, is discussed next. Some concluding comments follow in a final section.

A Cartel Explanation of the Early English Trading Companies

CARTEL FORMATION

The general pattern observable in the early English trading companies is that of the formation, by local merchants, of national cartels to engage in international trade. As Heckscher points out: "The work of unification in foreign trade was fairly easy, in so far as the medieval municipal economic system in all its local exclusiveness could not possibly be applied to foreign trade. Apart from the powerful North Italian cities, with towns and provinces under their direct control, it was on the whole impossible for the towns to exclude the competition of merchants from other towns in foreign markets. So the tendency towards common organization of a number of towns or their merchants came into being, and was accentuated by other specific phenomena" (1934, 1:326). Thus, the historians' interpretation of mercantilism is as a process of unification and development of nation-states, emanating, in the area of foreign trade, from the desire to suppress competition. In fact, combinations of towns represented nothing more than combinations of various local cartel arrangements, such as those enforced under the Statute of Artificers. The unification of nation-states—a primary theme of students of mercantilism—may then be interpreted as an extension of monopoly power from the local to the national level.

It is interesting to note that this extension of monopoly power has modern counterparts. For example, there is the Webb-Pomerene Law in the United States, which allows "qualified" domestic firms to form Webb associations (cartels) for the purpose of dealing in international trade. In theory the formation of these cartels should result in terms-of-trade advantages for the relevant domestic industry, since the industry can presumably exercise monopoly power in its international transactions. In practice, firms permitted to monopolize in this way have had little impact on the course of very competitive international markets but have used the Webb association, with its legislative exemption from antitrust, as a collusive setting from which to monopolize their domestic markets (Larson 1970). The analogy to the early trading companies should be clear. The early companies were expressions of monopoly power in towns and were used as a means to extend this power both domestically and internationally.

For the most part, in the mercantile period the English national cartels were formed by private initiative. Thus, "the English companies, it might . . . appear, were just as much a product of the state or of the monarchy as were the French; but in fact it was not so at all. The English companies owed their rise as well as their capital to private initiative. The king's good-will was manifested only in the attempt to share in the profits as far as possible, without making any contribution" (Heckscher 1934, 1:439). But the hand of the state was never very far behind private initiative. Often, the monarch made active investments. There is evidence that in the 1550's several very profitable, though nonmonopolized, partnerships were formed for the Africa trade. Scott (1951, 2:5) reports that the great gains from African expeditions could not be concealed, whereupon Elizabeth was brought into the partnerships in 1561. She provided capital in the form of four ships and provisions and was to receive a full one-third of the profits. When the Levant Company—formed to deal in the Mediterranean trade—was established in 1581, Elizabeth granted exclusive privileges to twenty merchants and invested or lent as much as half of the capital as partner (Scott 1951, 2:83–85).

Other forms of rent seeking via the sale of cartel restrictions were common. To take a specific example,

> The corporative business arrangements in the regulated companies are thus chiefly interesting as a proof that it was a short step, from a theoretical point of view, from the medieval corporations to the associations of capital. The interest in this relationship is not however entirely theoretical, for it is possible to trace an influence upon actual developments: e.g., Elizabeth (1560 and also later) on Gresham's advice, distrained on the outgoing fleets of the Merchant Adventurers and seized their cargoes of cloth, so as to force a loan from them which would cover the crown's debts on the continent and influence the exchanges in England's favour. The loan was considered one from the company itself, to be assessed upon its members [Heckscher 1934, 1:384].

In such a case the state stayed in the background and collected rents through "loans." Consequently, these companies fit into the rent-seeking predispositions of the times, whereby governments raised revenue by granting and enforcing monopoly privileges. This is, of course, not very different from the idea that firms granted Webb-Pomerene status might make large campaign contributions ("loans") to aspiring politicians. As we shall see, however, the form of state participation (franchising versus direct state control) had an important influence on the productive efficiency of the trading companies.

Cartels, then as now, were associations of firms (towns) maximizing joint profits via monopoly pricing, output restriction, and market allocations. The well-known problem with such business arrangements, once formed, relates to the matter of policing adherence to the agreement by the members. Since each cartel member faces a more elastic demand curve for its output with secret price reductions, cartel arrangements are often made unstable by a tendency of members to cheat on the agreement (Stigler 1964). Thus, once organized, the main task facing the foreign-trading cartels was to detect and sanction cheating on a joint price-output agreement. The various manifestations of this cartel-enforcement activity are interesting in their own right and, moreover, are illustrative of how cartels were organized and enforced in an era without antitrust sanctions against monopoly. Consider the cartel-enforcement activities of the English regulated companies.

CARTEL ENFORCEMENT

It was quite common for the merchant associations to have agents in the foreign markets that were important centers of exchange. The point of such activity seems basically to have been to observe the buying and selling activities of one's merchant colleagues in the cartel. Thus:

The English associations of merchants, on the other hand, had even their centre of activity abroad. In the years 1391 to 1408 a series of charters for various English corporations engaged in foreign trade were issued, and they described the merchants concerned as "sojourners" (*commorantes, commorantes et conversantes* respectively) in the foreign countries in question. The most important of these corporations was the famous Fellowship of Merchant(s) Adventurers or Merchant(s) Adventurers Company. It was governed from its Mart Town, that is, from its foreign office, down to its disappearance in Napoleonic times. . . . The second surviving medieval company in England was the Eastland Merchants or the Eastland Company. It is true that their centre was in London, not on the continent; but their continental office was allowed wide powers. When a less-known association trading with Andalusia obtained its charter in 1530, it referred to four Spanish cities as possible places for their meetings. The tradition therefore is clear [Heckscher 1934, 1:327–328].

Clearly, then, each cartel member stationed observers in the major markets through which cartel output flowed. In such a way enforcement of the cartel followed the course of trade, and the costs of violating the agreement for short-run gains were uniformly raised to all members.[1]

Cartel monitoring through agents or "factors" in foreign markets was not always wholly successful, as the experience of the Russia Company, a joint-stock association chartered by the crown in 1555, reveals. By 1568 there were allegations that "the factors were badly paid and that some of them embezzled the company's funds, others engaged in private trade, and a few even intrigued with the Dutch or interloping English merchants against the body that employed them" (Scott 1951, 2:42). As the earlier analysis in this book suggests, we expect malfeasance where agents are poorly paid, and the corruption of cartel agents was likely responsible for the early failures of the company. This situation added fuel to a later parliamentary assault on the company's exclusive privileges, but, in general, agent-monitors in foreign-trading centers appear to have been a very effective means of cartel enforcement.[2]

Another manifestation of cartel-enforcement activity by the English foreign-trade companies was their strong social codes. Heckscher's description of the situation is informative:

> From an economic point of view, the meticulous regulation of the lives of the merchants, their agents and apprentices is of minor importance, but throws light on the spirit of the system and expresses the striving after a supra-personal organization, embracing the whole individuality of its members. The members were never described as anything but "brethren", their wives were "sisters"; the "brethren" were to go together to church, to assist at weddings and burials. A whole chapter in the by-laws

---

[1]A close modern parallel to this practice of stationing cartel monitors in foreign market towns was the practice of the meat-packing industry in the United States from roughly 1910 to 1940. The meat packers effected a market-sharing agreement that was monitored via inspection of input purchases at the Chicago livestock market. See Nichols (1941) for this discussion.

[2]In 1604, in a wave of indignation at exclusive grants of monopoly, the Russia Company was charged with being a "monopoly within a monopoly," because fifteen directors (out of eighty stockholders) "had made one purse and stock of all," which is an indictment of the joint-stock arrangement. Further, Scott argued that "factors" were more adequately controlled under the regulated company form and that it took some time before the joint-stock type of organization learned to police their foreign-market representatives. There are, for instance, numerous examples of the high costs of policing malfeasance in the United East India Company in the early eighteenth century (Scott 1951, 2:197–198).

of the Merchant Adventurers is given up to punishments for indecent language, quarrels between brethren, fighting, drunkenness, card-playing, immorality, keeping of hunting dogs and so on. It was also unlawful to enter the porter's lodge on the arrival of the post—instead, letters were to be received at his window outside the lodge; further no one was to carry through the streets any more than could be decently held under the arm or in the sleeve—infringements of any of these carrying fines of different severity. The same rules are to be found in the sister organization, though typically enough masters were excepted from the prohibition against "undecent speeches or words of reproach or discredit" when they upbraided their apprentices and paid servants. Apprentices were the children of the large family and were treated as such [1934, 1:380].

Although these codes could have been motivated by general social or religious considerations, their function seems to have been to make it virtually impossible for cartel members to have an opportunity to cheat on the agreement. Why else, for example, would mail be monitored within these associations, as Heckscher indicates, if not to check for violations of the cartel agreement? Thus, from the point of view of cartel enforcement, the detailed regulation of the lives of cartel members was not of minor economic importance, as Heckscher seems to think. The social codes of these trading associations were implicit cartel-monitoring devices dispersing the costs of enforcement over all the cartel members and their families.

Another interesting manifestation of cartel-enforcement activity in the early companies was the severe membership restrictions on former retailers. Heckscher describes these restrictions: "The new state of affairs was given clear expression in the fact that members of the regulated companies were prohibited from devoting themselves to retail trading. In exceptionally strict cases it was even forbidden to accept people as members who had at any time been retailers. It became a rule that the members had to be 'mere merchants' " (1934, 1:378). In the case of the London merchants, Heckscher continues,

Any person who had once been a retailer had to declare in writing one year before his admission to the organization, that he wished to renounce retail trading or shopkeeping, and he was not allowed to return to it within five years; all this on pain of heavy fines for infringement. The 1605 charter for the Levant Company and the 1611 charter for merchants trading with France went even farther. For a member to be a retailer was made to be as much a crime as "offences and the practices of evil demeanour", the punishment for which was expulsion. The rules had to be considerably toned down for the provincial cities; but the endeavour to erect a barrier between wholesale and above all maritime trade on the one hand and handicraft and retail trade on the other dominated the regulated companies throughout their existence, and was, for instance, intensified in the Merchant Adventurers by governmental ordinances of 1634 and 1643 [1934, 1:379].

Heckscher offers no explanation for the separation of retailers from merchants, but it is clear that such separation was a device for controlling incentives to cheat on the cartel. A former retailer would have had numerous market contacts from his previous sales experience and would have been in a relatively advantageous position to make "illicit" sales. A ban on former retailers made perfectly good economic sense from the point of view of cartel management.

A final manifestation of cartel enforcement concerns the cartel policy of common shipping through and the general dominance of London as a port. The nature of the provisions for common shipping are clear in the following quotation from Heckscher:

> The rights of the local branches to ship independently were, even in other ways, most curiously treated in the Merchant Adventurers' by-laws. It is true that the clauses did not prohibit the use of other ports than London, and Newcastle even enjoyed special facilities for its goods, which differed somewhat from those of the London branch. But with this exception, the clauses were occupied almost exclusively with shipping from the London office. The codification of 1608 expressly stipulated that no prescriptions relating to shipping could be allowed without the advice of the London members. On the ground that decisions on the freighting of common ships must be kept under strict control of officials, members "of whatsoever place or port of England" were also forbidden to remove a commodity from London or the surrounding district, once they had brought it in. In the words of Wheeler (1601) who was the force behind the codification, "the most part of the commodities which the Merchants Adventurers carry out of the Realm, being shipped in appointed ships at London." In other words, the common shipping of the company in his day played a large part in its affairs. There was thus an unmistakable desire on the part of the Merchant Adventurers to concentrate trade and shipping in London [1934, 1:427].

Common shipping was still another means of controlling cheating on the cartel arrangement, and such a policy lowered the costs to cartel managers of policing cartel transactions.[3] The focus on London as a central port for cartel management, moreover, must have been due to lower costs of cartel operations there. Heckscher, though generally confusing the issue of London's dominance by viewing the issue in broad social and political terms, hints at our analysis in the following passage:

The twofold origin of the animosity and the jealousy towards London, displayed from the start by the merchants and shipowners of the "outports", complicates the survey of the situation. On the one hand the unorganized traders, the provincial "interlopers", tried their utmost to make life unpleasant for their officially favoured competitors in London. On the other hand, there was the opposition between the provincial and the metropolitan members of the organizations themselves. This distinction is frequently overlooked; but the very fact that it could be overlooked arouses the suspicion that the interest of London was largely a company interest, in other words that the companies' advantage as such involved the favouring of London at the expense of the provinces. At the same time it must not be assumed that no distinction was made between these two kinds of opposition, and in fact the organized merchants in the provinces sometimes explicitly distinguished between their fight with the directors of their own company in London and the interlopers' fight with the companies as such [1934, 1:418].

Heckscher seems to argue that there was something akin to a regional-development fight surrounding the matter of London's dominance as a port. Heckscher's view is certainly partially correct, but the economic basis of the dominance of London was more likely the lower costs of centralizing cartel operations in that city.

All of these aspects of cartel enforcement are obvious manifestations of cartel agreements. The point is that policing these agreements, which also means policing the cartel, is costly but efficient from the cartel's point of view. The internally efficient cartel will use efficient policing devices out of the whole array of possible devices.

[3]Other forms of cheating were proscribed in the details of charters. Thus, in a patent to Sir Nicholas Crisp for the Company of Merchants trading to Guinea (1630), it was provided that no Englishman, save the patentees, was allowed to import any merchandise produced in Africa. The reason for the provision was to end indirect importation of such commodities through European countries (Scott 1951, 2:14).

OUTPUT ASSIGNMENT IN THE CARTEL

A problem plaguing any cartel is how to allocate production among members. The problem is especially difficult when member firms have different costs of production. Heckscher aptly characterizes the nature of the output-assignment problem in the early trading cartels: "On the whole, however, the system was rather more refined, and one of its usual tenets was the limitation of the total number of merchants and their sales, and the division of the total sales among various merchants by limiting the amounts which any merchant might ship, so that "the rich" might not "eat out the poor". It was just this which was usually named "stint", and with the Merchant Adventurers it played a specially important role" (1934, 1: 381).

The provision that "the rich might not eat out the poor" seems to be nothing more than an output-assignment rule in trading cartels. By analogy, the "rich" correspond to low-cost firms and the "poor" to high-cost firms. While a fully rationalized cartel would allocate the profit-maximizing output according to the marginal costs of its members, these early cartels evidently had as much trouble achieving full rationalization as do modern cartels. The difficulty was (is) perhaps due to the fact that the prospect of shutting down—if one happens to be a relatively high-cost producer—is the functional equivalent to unilateral disarmament. Where the costs of reentry are high, the probability of being double-crossed by the low-cost firms that would remain in production becomes substantial. Most cartels thus have rules whereby all firms continue to produce. Rich (low-cost) firms do not eat out the poor (high-cost) firms, albeit cartel profits are not strictly maximized as a result.[4]

CARTEL FORMATION, AGAIN

We have, in a way, put the cart before the horse by focusing first on the various ways in which the early companies enforced their cartel agreements and allocated production among members, rather

---

[4]The genuine mystery is why markets for production rights within cartels do not generally emerge. Such a market would facilitate trade in production rights between low- and high-cost firms, and cartel profitability would be enhanced as a result. See Maloney and McCormick (1980) for an instructive analysis of this problem.

than on the difficulties of forming the cartel. There is a good reason for this order of discussion, however, since there is no documentation of negotiations among various town merchants forming these early cartels. We do know, in general, that the associations of town merchants devised a very efficient form of collusion—the common selling agency. Coupled with various devices to control cheating on agreements discussed above, a common sales agency is an extremely effective means of private cartel management.[5] Heckscher understood this basic point quite clearly: "They sometimes took over the products of their members and put credits to their accounts, obliging the traders to deliver their goods only to the corporation warehouses, corresponding roughly to the arrangement in a modern cartel with a common selling syndicate" (1934, 1:383). We might also note that the general efficiency of collusive arrangements in this period was to be expected in a setting where cartels were not only legal, but were actively encouraged by state authorities who stood to gain revenues from the creation of monopoly rents.

SUMMARY

Heckscher's interests in recounting the history of the early companies were substantially broader, in general, than our interest in their cartel activities. Heckscher gave a starring role to the grand theme of mercantilism as a unifying force that created the nation-state. In this context Heckscher studied the impact of the early companies on unification and was not concerned with an interpretation from the standpoint of positive-economic theory. We view the history of the early English companies in a somewhat different light. The movement to unified trading companies was monopolistically inspired, and the various details of social history that followed the formation of these companies were manifestations of cartel activity.

---

[5]This is not to say, of course, that the efficiency and profitability of these cartels was not constantly challenged by the activities of illegal competitors or interlopers. "Smuggling," then and now, is a predictable response to protected markets. A number of patentees, such as Sir Nicholas Crisp, who founded a company for the Africa trade in 1630, got their franchises by successfully challenging the privileges of preceding companies. When it was in the crown's interest, moreover, interlopers received support from the monarchy itself. Such was the case when James I—irritated at having been refused a "loan" of £10,000 from the London East India Company—supported a rival association (Courten's Association) for his own profit (see Scott 1951, 2:112–116).

Comparative Economic Performance of the Foreign-Trading Companies

The comparative economic performance of the foreign-trading companies in several of the mercantile economies is surveyed by Heckscher. His interest in this subject is, again, not in the positive-economic aspects of this problem but in its relation to broader issues of the mercantilist era. Our interest is in the economic explanations for the observable differences in the operations of companies in the various countries.

Our argument essentially is that the economic performance of the trading companies in the mercantile economies was directly related to the degree of state involvement in the affairs of these enterprises. The efficiency of the Dutch companies was widely admired and rested on the private and competitive nature of these enterprises. The Portuguese and Spanish companies were notoriously inefficient, and they will be characterized as either public enterprises or as massive sole proprietorships owned solely by the king and queen. The (mainly government-owned) French companies were organized for political objectives. The English cartels seemed to operate on an efficient compromise. The crown granted the relevant monopoly trading privilege in return for what amounted to a monopoly-franchise fee from the companies in the form of loans, but the companies (cartels) were organized and operated by private initiative.

THE DUTCH COMPANIES

Heckscher characterizes the Dutch companies as paradoxical. In his words, "the Netherlands were the most hated, and yet the most admired and envied commercial nation of the 17th century." The Dutch were, by far, the most efficient seafarers and cargo transporters of that century. Nonetheless, while the Netherlands were the seeming ideal of all mercantilists, they "were yet at the same time less affected by mercantilist tendencies than most other countries" (1934, 1:351). Heckscher attempts to dismiss this paradoxical observation on the grounds of "the national characteristics of the people" (1934, 1:353). While the personal initiative of the Dutch people is undoubtedly an important reason for the efficiency of their trading companies, we do not think that this a satisfactory economic explanation for the paradox that Heckscher poses.

Rather, we see the efficiency of the Dutch companies as stemming from two basic sources. First, in the early period of the trading companies, the Dutch towns experienced great difficulties in organizing a national cartel for the purpose of dealing in foreign trade. These difficulties seemed to be typical of those normally associated with cartel formation. Thus, "the 'directions' were all purely local institutions set up by the towns. The hostility between the 'directions' of various cities was often very keen, although certain attempts were made to induce them to co-operate. It is true that the extent of this hostility was greatly limited in practice by the overwhelming preponderance of Amsterdam both in the sea trade and in the shipping of the Netherlands. But it illustrated the ineradicable particularism, which had hardly been attacked at all seriously, in the conglomeration of cities and territories comprehended in the sometimes almost ironical name of the United Provinces—a particularism which scorned all mercantilist efforts at unification" (Heckscher 1934, 1:355).

Dutch particularism and local hostilities noted by Heckscher can here be interpreted as enhancing competition, in the sense that they made cartel formation more difficult, while, at the same time, making competition more prevalent among the merchants in the Dutch towns. While these hostilities and difficulties were certainly embedded in the characteristics of the Dutch peoples, it seems sensible as an economic hypothesis to ascribe the efficiency of the Dutch companies to the costs of cartel formation and to the consequent persistence of competitive pressures. Thus, for example, Heckscher's (1:352) discussion of the ability of the early Dutch companies to make do with fewer and simpler organizations than the comparable companies in other countries probably reflects the discipline of competition more than anything else. Also, purely technological explanations of superior Dutch efficiencies (for example, the well-known fact that they built lower-cost ships) can be seen as a manifestation of competitive pressures.

Dutch towns eventually overcame difficulties of cartel formation and united into a national trading company. Again, Heckscher describes this process:

The various authorities, both municipal and provincial, as well as the States General were extremely perturbed by this competition in their East India trade, partly because they saw in it a danger for the very existence of this trade, but also for political and military reasons, since it prevented a united front being formed against the king of Spain, who at that time was also king of Portugal and thus master of the East Indian waters. Repeated attempts were made to unite the various interests. An amalgamation of the six companies which had their seats in Amsterdam also came into being, but it was of little avail, for the Zeeland merchants, who were always suspicious of the Holland merchants, kept themselves aloof and united in opposition to the Holland enterprises. Such being the situation, it was only the States General which could help. The work of unification was thrown on to the shoulders of the foremost Dutch statesman of the time, Oldenbarnevelt. After involved negotiations, promoted by the States General, all the existing enterprises were, with one negligible exception, amalgamated to form the "united" East India Company in 1602, eight years after the birth of the first company. One of the most powerful forces in the colonial history of Europe for the next two centuries was thus created [1934, 1:356].

Thus, the East India Company was formed with some aid from the state, and, as documented by Heckscher and others, it became one of the most efficient national trading companies of the mercantile era. A second basic consideration, therefore, in understanding the effectiveness of the Dutch companies over this period concerns how the efficiency of the precartel Dutch companies was carried over to the East India Company.

An uncomplicated answer is that the forces of distrust and competitiveness among the precartel companies inhered in the national cartel arrangement of the Dutch, and these forces put considerable pressure on the various local units in the cartel to behave efficiently. For example, consider the great interest manifested in sharing schemes for cartel costs and returns in the following quotation:

Functioning as the principal organs of the company and with far-reaching authority were six chambers, as they were called, organized on a purely local basis. The greatest and by far the most important of them all was that of Amsterdam, the next that of the province Zeeland, and the remaining four those of Maas and the towns of the "northern quarter",

Delft, Rotterdam, Hoorn and Enkhuizen. From the outset these chambers had each contributed a definite part of the company's capital and later too had to arrange for the distribution of dividends to the various shareholders. They had to bear a definite proportionate share of all the costs (one-half, one-quarter and one-sixteenth respectively, Art. 1 of the charter). For example, when it was arranged that the management in India receive annually eight *legger* of Rhine wine, the chambers had to contribute eight, four and one *legger* each, respectively. The equipment of the ships and the procuring of cargoes, provisions and arms, as well as the actual building of the ships all devolved upon the individual chambers. The ships had eventually to return to those chambers from which they had departed (Art. 12). They had to bring back "returns", that is Indian products, for the chamber which had equipped the ship as well as for the others. The orders for these "returns" were distributed among the chambers, and they each had to sell the goods received, but all on the common account of the company. The administration in India belonged indeed to the company as a whole, but, with the exception of the chief officials, it was recruited by nomination, made independently by the individual chambers whose hands were tied only in certain matters of secondary importance, and which moreover often treated with indifference the few legal limitations that had been laid down [Heckscher 1934, 1:362].

The concern, illustrated here, about schemes for the allocation of costs and returns within the cartel was presumably a reflection of the distrust among former competitors. Such apprehensions about business colleagues led to investments in the careful monitoring of co-partners' behavior. These apprehensions, moreover, established a cartel administrative system that made cheating on the cartel costly and that appears to have tailored cartel output to each local unit's marginal cost ("the ships had eventually to return to those chambers from which they had departed"). Distrust among former competitors, in other words, serves as an explanation of the efficiency of the Dutch foreign-trading cartel.

A little hostility went a long way, as it were, in promoting economic efficiency in Dutch foreign trade in this era. If such competitiveness is a characteristic of the Dutch people, we hold that it is also a normal characteristic of most people. Our analysis of the impact of competition on economic organization thus offers a more familiar and useful route to the understanding of the commercial success of the mercantile Dutch than that offered by Heckscher.

THE PORTUGUESE AND SPANISH COMPANIES

The state-owned-and-operated trading companies of Portugal and Spain reflect the opposite extreme from the Dutch experience. In these cases the crown completely financed the companies and was the sole residual claimant in the returns of their trading adventures. In effect, the trading companies of Portugal and Spain may be characterized in two ways.

First, they may be seen as monopolistically inspired public enterprises. When viewed as public enterprises, the results are entirely predictable. For example,

On the return to Portugal the goods were then sold to merchants. This rule, though stringent in theory, was widely infringed in fact, through the private trade carried on by officials and the ship's crew. Such private trade was originally permitted to a small extent in accordance with the practice of former times, but it came to such a pass that eventually whole vessels were on occasions laden with the captain's own goods. The officials always took good care that their own private and illicit trading in India and at home should take precedence over the lawful trade. The work of Sir William Hunter, in fact, based on official English transcriptions of the materials in Portuguese archives, gives the impression that the illicit trade was even greater than that of the state. . . . This, the most far-reaching attempt of all to institute pure state trading, did not encourage imitation [Heckscher 1934, 1:342].

As illustrated here, managerial shirking abounded in the Portuguese companies, a result that would come as no surprise to the modern economist familiar with the property-rights theory of the firm (Alchian and Demsetz 1972). Such behavior flows naturally from the absence of market competition and from the absence of well-defined and exchangeable property rights in public enterprises (Davies 1971). Production without property rights characterized the Portuguese and Spanish state trading companies, and general inefficiency in these firms followed as a direct economic consequence.

There is yet another, and perhaps more accurate, manner in which the Portuguese and Spanish companies may be characterized. Instead of being seen as public enterprises—owned by everyone and hence by no one—the companies might be viewed as large monopolies operated as sole proprietorships. The sole proprietor in this case was the monarchy. Under such an interpretation, the inefficiencies observed would be seen to have emerged for classical economic reasons. Where the king and queen were both the sole residual claimants and monopolists, span of control and managerial diseconomies would have been massive and would have led to large-firm inefficiencies. Either characterization of the Spanish and Portuguese enterprises predicts the results described by mercantile writers in this area.

THE FRENCH COMPANIES

The French were as poor at international rent seeking as they were expert in maintaining incredibly efficient internal regulations. As mentioned earlier, the Dutch were the undisputed masters of the "carrying trade" throughout the first three-quarters of the seventeenth century. Dutch hegemony included the European trade with Russia, a vast carrying trade between the Baltic nations and Spain and Portugal, and trade with the West Indies (at least for a time), not to mention the establishment of Amsterdam as the credit and money-market center of Europe. Both the English and the French attempted to contain the Dutch, but, from an economic point of view at least, sponsored efforts in this area were extremely costly. Most of the French experience in international "company formation" may be interpreted as an aggressive policy to teach the Dutch a lesson and to restrict their international influence. Rightly or wrongly, it seems, the French viewed the Dutch as responsible for long-term stagnation in the French economy. Brief examination of two of Colbert's major constructions in this area, the French West India Company and the Company of the North, yields some insights into the nature of French foreign-trading companies.

The East India and West India companies were linked with French colonization efforts, while the Company of the North was not. Nonetheless, all appear to have been financial disasters, supported in large measure by the treasury of Louis XIV and France. The West India Company was formed to oust the Dutch from the carrying trade in the French island possessions in the West Indies. Colbert envisioned great economies from a French monopoly over this trade, especially with regard to the large sugar trade with France and to the marketing of French linen in the new world. Thus, Colbert sought to set up, under one monopoly organization, trade with the West Indies, South America, Canada, and West Africa, subsequently buying out most of the private proprietors granted monopoly rights before 1665. Stock subscriptions were solicited between 1664 and 1669, with over five and one-half million *livres* collected for capital. But with 54 percent contributed by the king and with most of the rest pledged by government officials and not merchants, the "corporation" was more a government monopoly than a mercantile enterprise. As in the Spanish and Portuguese companies, this form of enterprise, because of the lack of clearly defined property rights within the firm, is the root explanation for the subsequent and costly inefficiencies of the French companies.

The West India Company was a debacle from the beginning. In 1664 a royal decree excluded the Dutch from trading in the French colonies, but because of the irregularities of supplies and high prices, the French colonists hated the company, on occasion rioting against it, and wanted the Dutch to return. Financial problems also beset the company, which was kept in business by treasury advances authorized by Colbert. In 1666 island wars with England, together with huge losses of ships, cargo, and trade unconnected with the English disputes, led Colbert gradually to abandon the company.

Several aspects of the West India Company's fate are interesting. Colbert had set up the company to be run by a stock-holding chamber of directors in Paris and by decentralized boards of directors and governors in France and in the colonies (see Cole 1939, 1:3–5, for details). But there is some evidence of profit taking and shirking by those in control. When it became apparent that the company could not handle the basic requisites of trade to the colonies, especially during wartime in 1666, private French traders (and sometimes the Dutch as well) were let in, but with passports granted to the private firms by the company itself. Clearly, this opened the door to rent seeking by company officials, and there is evidence of such behavior: Colbert himself took over the right to grant licenses to private traders in an effort to prevent favoritism by the company.

Moreover, while Colbert gradually encouraged private French merchants to take over the West Indies trade, he did attempt to reorganize the company along more efficient lines in 1669. In the reorganization proceedings, each member of the board of directors was given specific duties and told to work on company business between four P.M. and seven P.M. four days a week. However, since returns of company directors were not directly linked to their efforts on behalf of the company and since returns were not based upon performance (a stockholders' dividend out of the *royal* treasury was declared in January, 1669, to solicit new investments), free riding and rent seeking by the directors was to be expected.

Another feature of the West India trade made its continuation precarious. Though the West Indies Company was a huge investment, the French were unwilling or unable to expend enough resources to contain the interloping of private traders and Dutch slave and live-stock trade. Since the services of the company were notoriously in-efficient and did not satisfy the colonists, the situation was ripe for outright avoidance of the law (smuggling) and for malfeasance by island officials and even by members of the company. At bottom, the French did in fact significantly displace Dutch trade in the French West Indies, but the displacement appears to have been largely by private traders. Whatever impact the West India Company had on this (largely) political feat, France paid dearly in terms of wasted resources.

Another (but non-colony-related) attempt to "get the Dutch" was the French attempt to move in on the Dutch carrying trade (of mainly French products) to northern Europe. But at this the French were utterly inept. Colbert tried to rouse businessmen's interests in the project, and the Company of the North was founded with mo-nopoly privileges in 1669. Again, a central board of directors was appointed, with local boards in the trading cities, and the king in-vested well over one-third of the capital, together with escorts and naval protection for the company's ships. This time, however, trade was to be partly subsidized by government demand for naval supplies and by reciprocal exports of French goods and goods from the West Indies. But by 1671 Dutch competition was fierce, trade restrictions and counter-restrictions were invoked in Franco-Dutch political con-frontations, and the company had spent all of its capital and had to be rescued by the royal treasury. The French could not get a foothold on the Dutch carrying trade between Spain and Portugal and the Baltic, and the entire experiment collapsed when open war broke out between the French and the Dutch in 1672. The Company of the North was liquidated, de facto at least, between 1673 and 1677, to become another example of disastrous political and economic war-fare with the Dutch, who simply out-competed the French. As we have stressed in this section, the reason for this result resides primarily in the competitive atmosphere and private-ownership structure of the Dutch companies compared with the state financing and state direction of the French companies.

THE ENGLISH COMPANIES

Our final case for comparative analysis is the "regulated" trading companies in England, introduced earlier in this chapter. These may have been the most interesting of the foreign-trading companies, in terms of the institutional arrangements under which they operated. As pointed out previously, these cartels were formed by private initiative under the auspices of a monopoly grant from the crown, and the state sought to share in the consequent monopoly rents through what was the functional equivalent of monopoly franchising. In fact, the English regulated companies appear to represent an historical example relevant to a modern theoretical argument about monopoly franchising (Demsetz 1968). Before turning to the details of the analysis, however, let us examine how Heckscher describes the institutional milieu of the English companies:

> The formal relationship between the companies and the state consisted in this, that the state paid for the advantages it received from the companies by issuing charters. But the actual profit derived from the company charters was twofold, and there was an important difference between the two.
> One part of the benefit was made up of a monopoly, in the usual sense of the word—exclusive rights granted to the companies in their various fields of activity. The monopoly, of course, was employed by its owner to demand higher prices than he would otherwise have been able to get, which meant, in effect, that the customers paid for the credit which the state had secured through the companies. The system thus involved an indirect taxation of consumers' goods in the financial interests of the state. It was indirect taxation of consumption by means of a monopoly, not in the hands of the state but wielded by private individuals. . . . The second aspect was of a totally different kind, consisting as it did in the right to corporative status. It might appear as though the state in this case granted a favour costing nothing at all and as though the companies gained something for which no one had to pay; but that is a mistake. Where the actual advantage lay was in the fact that the arrangement was not extended to everybody. The state could demand payment in return for its permission to form corporative associations, simply because it withheld the same privilege from all the other concerns which could

have made use of it. In reality these privileges, too, were exploited as private monopolies by the state for fiscal ends. The general effect on economic life and on the consumers was that the other non-corporative undertakings did not provide the public with as good a service as they might have done had they been allowed a corporative status; and consequently the privileged enterprises made the public pay not only for their specific privileges, but also for their more suitable organization. For this reason they were prepared to pay the Crown for these advantages by allowing it favourable terms for loans [1934, 1:441–442].

The system under which the foreign-trading cartels operated in mercantile England was quite similar to Demsetz's (1968) proposal for franchising natural monopolies. Demsetz suggested that the formal regulation of natural monopolies might be rendered unnecessary were government to allow "rivalrous competitors" to bid for the exclusive right to supply the good or service over some indefinite "contract" period. The existence of natural monopoly does not imply a monopoly price and output in this system, assuming an elastic supply of potential bidders and prohibitive collusion costs on the part of potential suppliers.[6] Rather, the result of the Demsetz bidding scheme is that the firm with the lowest average-cost curve will win the contract and will supply the market at an average-cost price. The state is involved in this process only to the minimal extent of running the franchising or contracting procedure. Direct regulation of the natural monopoly to seek to get the firm to charge an average-cost price, with all its incumbent problems, is avoided. Moreover, the Demsetz result does not rely on the existence of a natural monopoly; it can be applied regardless of the cost conditions that are present among the firms bidding for the contract.

Returning to the English trading companies, the analogy to monopoly franchising is clear. Groups of merchants bought their monopoly privileges by making "loans" to the state. So long as this process of selling monopoly rights was reasonably competitive, and the historical accounts of court intrigues and cabals during this era suggest that it was, this system of establishing foreign-trading companies would have had a wholesome impact on enterprise efficiency,

---

[6]There are a number of problems in the practical implementation of this plan; for a discussion of some of these issues, see Williamson (1976) and Crain and Ekelund (1976).

as predicted by the Demsetz model.[7] Moreover, the state was not involved in a direct way in the operation of these firms, as it was in the Portuguese and Spanish cases (and somewhat in the French case), and the fact that the monopoly rights were auctioned off tended to ensure that the most efficient "monopolist" (collection of merchants) won the bidding competition for the monopoly right. This system of "competition for the field" thus maximized the franchise fees received by the state and enhanced the economic efficiency of the English trading companies.

SUMMARY

Across the mercantile economies the following pattern of enterprise efficiency in foreign-trading companies emerges. The Dutch developed more competitive and efficient trading companies. Moreover, that there was apparently little state involvement further enhanced the effectiveness of their operations. When the Dutch formed a national trading cartel (the East India Company), competitive pressures continued to manifest themselves in the promotion of an efficient cartel operation. The Portuguese and Spanish adopted pure state trading companies or very large "single proprietorships" sponsored by royal authorities, resulting in the predictable enterprise inefficiencies that come about as the result of production without property or ownership rights and the lack of competitive pressures. Some of these similar pressures appear to have been operative in the French experience with foreign-trading companies, which were only very nominally private in character. Finally, the English happened upon an efficient compromise, wherein private interests formed the trading cartels and bid for the pertinent monopoly right from the crown. The crown captured the monopoly rents, and the most efficient firm won the "contract" to operate the trading company.

[7]This method of auctioning off monopoly rights to maximize state returns may have played an important role in the colonizing and exploratory adventures of England, as well as in the fishery and mineral exploitations of the crown. There is evidence that a similar plan was instituted by Cromwell in 1653 for the provision of postal services (see Priest 1975, pp. 36–37 and footnote 24).

The Rise of the Joint-Stock Companies in England
Mercantile Origins of the Corporation

The modern corporate form of business organization evolved over many centuries, and despite a large body of historical research its origins are still obscure. Why, then, was the corporation invented? The early joint-stock companies in England embodied an important change in contractual form. As noted in the introduction to this chapter, scholars have hypothesized that these corporations evolved in response to an exogenous increase in the demand for capital by the early foreign-trading companies. Our complementary, supply-side hypothesis stresses the advantages that more readily transferable rights held for the owner-managers of these early companies. These two hypotheses and the historical evidence on their relative importance will help us explain the emergence of the corporate form of economic organization.

THE CONVENTIONAL WISDOM

The foreign-trading companies in England were essentially merchant cartels that had received charters from the crown to engage in trade with specified countries. The rules devised to govern these cartels were extensive and detailed, and they were thus designated as regulated companies. The early public joint-stock companies in England (circa 1553) were, predictably, little different in substance from the regulated companies. The standard hypothesis explaining the rise of joint-stock companies in England is that contractual provisions of these companies, especially limited liability, enabled them to raise capital more readily than the regulated companies. This argument was taken as a given by the classical writers, as it is by contemporary economic historians (Clough and Rapp 1975, p. 152; Tuma 1971, p. 297). To J. S. Mill for example, the capital-accumulative aspect was of primary importance: "Production on a large scale is greatly promoted by the practice of forming a large capital by the combination of many small contributions; or, in other words, by the formation of joint stock companies. The advantages of the joint stock principle are numerous and important. In the first place, *many undertakings require an amount of capital*

beyond the means of the richest individual or private partnership"
(1965, p. 137). Further, in a classic work on the mercantile companies, W. R. Scott (1951) argues that "the joint-stock company
was no more than the ready means for improving production by
arranging for the ready inflow of capital" (1:442. See also Scott's
chapter 21).

The analytical basis for Scott's hypothesis was an exogenous
increase in demand for capital by the regulated companies, which
could only be accommodated by a change in legal form. There is
certainly some truth to the argument that the trading companies'
demand for capital increased over time. The early expeditions by
the trading companies were essentially hand-to-mouth affairs. Each
expedition was financed independently, to be decomposed into returns at the voyage's end. It is quite reasonable for writers to argue
that these companies required a certain amount of infrastructure to
carry on foreign trade on an ongoing basis as trade routes and business practices became more regular over the period. For example,
warehouses became necessary to manage inventories at home and
abroad.

There is thus nothing inherently incorrect in the "classical"
view that as the trading companies grew their demand for capital also
grew. To us, however, this cannot be the whole story of the evolution
of the corporate form. The primary shortcoming is that it is a purely
demand-driven explanation, and, as such, it excludes some important
supply-side considerations. Moreover, as a single explanatory hypothesis, the demand-for-capital argument neglects some crucial market
functions. For example, with respect to debt capital (and in these
closely held companies this appears to have been the major method
of raising capital), market forces would have been working to negate
the capital-raising argument. A change in legal form from a closely
held company, wherein the wealth of partners was mutually liable,
to a joint-stock company with limited liability would not have dramatically affected the supply side of the loan market, that is, the terms
on which companies could borrow (see Meiners, Mofsky, and Tollison 1979). The early joint-stock companies were still closely held;
partner-stockholders put up the same loan collateral (for example,
personal assets) as before or faced higher interest rates. Thus, the

cost of capital to the early companies should have been roughly the same under either contractual arrangement.

PROPERTY RIGHTS IN THE EARLY COMPANIES

The English regulated companies, as we have stressed, were associations of merchants who colluded to restrict competition among the towns in international trade. These cartels, legally sanctioned and encouraged by state authorities, generally operated with great effectiveness.[8] However, one aspect of their operations was troublesome: sustaining the economic organization over time as cartel owner-managers retired or otherwise sought to leave the organization. The regulated companies solved this problem in the way that most family firms solve it—by passing on cartel rights within the family. Heckscher offers some of the flavor of this process: "The companies could not possibly remain open to everyone, quite irrespective of whether they admitted merchants from every city or not. This followed from its principle of limiting competition which was inherent in its medieval origins. Many facts can be adduced to substantiate the point. The fine was often extortionate. In the Merchant Adventurers' Company, according to its codified by-laws of 1608, it was no less than £200 sterling for 'redemptioners', i.e. those who were not sons or apprentices of members" (1934, 1:387).

Primarily, of course, the apprenticeship system was designed to restrict entry and create monopoly rents for cartel members. But submerged in the background of this process was the issue of ensuring the continuity and efficiency of the firm's operation over time. As we see it, this issue telescopes to a question of the transferability of property rights in these cartels.[9] In the early regulated companies,

---

[8]A general point seems relevant here: a very basic reason for any "firm"—partnership or joint-stock company—to emerge in a rent-seeking world is that lobbying costs are thereby reduced. Coalescence for production, i.e., establishment of a "firm," reduces the potential for free-riding on the firm's lobbying expenditures. The cost of procuring government protection from the firm's viewpoint is thus reduced.

[9]Transferable property rights play a central role in the explanation of the evolution and dissipation of peasant society in England. For a consideration of the origins of transferable property rights in this broad setting see Macfarlane (1978).

and the African trade provides an excellent example (Scott 1951, 2:5–8), the property rights of owner-managers were difficult to transfer. There was no active capital market where such rights could be traded, and, moreover, there was the usual difficulty associated with partnerships—a partner's exit from the firm was restricted by the requirement that a new partner be satisfactory to those partners remaining in the firm. A partner thus maintained his stake in the cartel by staying in the firm or by keeping the relevant property rights in the family. The lack of easily transferable property rights made it efficient for the owner-managers to retain their cartel rights within their families.[10]

Corporate primogeniture, however, led to an economic problem for the cartel, for there was no guarantee that sons, grandsons, or nephews (in the case of no male issue) would constitute the most effective set of cartel owner-managers. Thus, if these rights could be more readily traded, cartel profitability would be enhanced over the long run. That important point follows because the salable cartel rights would then flow to their highest-valued uses, that is, to those who had a comparative advantage in cartel management. Our basic hypothesis about the invention of the corporation is straightforward. The cartel owner-managers had wealth-maximizing incentives to seek the development of a legal form of organization under which they could more easily trade their property rights in these firms. Such a system promoted greater efficiency in the market for the managers of state-chartered monopoly rights.

There are several related advantages of more readily tradable property rights that could have been important in the adaptation of economic organization to the joint-stock form. First, cartel management in the early companies may be viewed as a team-production process (Alchian and Demsetz 1972). Some device must be found in this setting to control incentives for cartel managers to shirk and free-ride off the managerial efforts of their colleagues. Market competition by alternative managers provided an obvious source of dis-

---

[10]That is to say, nepotism is sometimes an efficient form of behavior. We hypothesize that in early companies such behavior derived from monopoly positions that were not easily marketable. In a modern setting we might expect disproportionate numbers of the children of doctors, lawyers, politicians, and local businessmen to remain in the family firm for quite similar reasons.

cipline, but such forces were attenuated by the monopolistic and closely held character of these companies. Alternatively, these firms could have developed profit-sharing arrangements that tailored rewards to managerial productivity. However, where cartel managerial efforts are a team-production process and separate managerial inputs cannot be easily disentangled, such a profit-sharing scheme would not be easy to devise. A capital market, however, which went hand-in-hand with the joint-stock form, wherein firms' shares could be more easily traded, provided a mechanism external to the firm through which the behavior of the cartel owner-managers could be disciplined and monitored. Thus, an auxiliary and supporting explanation for the emergence of the corporation, also emanating from the supply side, is that more easily tradable property rights in the early companies provided an external system of discipline for cartel management. Second, a general argument developed by Demsetz (1967) and Jensen and Meckling (1976)—quite similar in spirit to our own—is that the advantage of a limited-liability provision is not that it exposes the investor to less risk, but that it reduces certain relevant transaction costs for the investor (such as monitoring the course of co-partners' net wealth and their commitments on behalf of the firm). Rather than bear these costs, investors pay a higher interest rate in a regime of limited liability in which it is relatively easier to exchange shares. Finally, share transferability also permitted owners and managers to specialize. Whether this functional separation (and the incentive structure it creates) increases or decreases firm efficiency remains, of course, a matter of debate. Limited liability, however, may be seen as a contractual device designed to mitigate any consequent divergence of interest between owners and managers.

THE HISTORICAL CASE FOR THE PROPERTY-RIGHTS ARGUMENT

Most accounts of the early companies by historians emphasize the demand-for-capital explanation of the rise of the joint-stock form. As we have pointed out, the property-rights argument that we advance does not contradict the capital-raising argument. There is, however, a question of the emphasis to be given to each argument. In this section we present some evidence on the relative importance of the two approaches in explaining the invention of the joint-stock corporation.

In assessing the importance of the demand-for-capital argument, we must keep in mind that the organization of early joint-stock companies was almost identical to that of the regulated companies. Both types of firms existed coincidentally; both were state-chartered monopolies; both were closely held firms. Heckscher makes this point quite clearly:

This connection was also expressed in the fact that the pronounced medieval character of the trading bodies was not merely confined to the regulated companies, but was also extended to the capital associations. . . . A pamphlet published as late as 1702 emphasized that "the general intent and end of all civil incorporations is for better government, either general or special", i.e. the same argument as that commonly adduced for the legality of the gilds; and to illustrate the point, its author quoted indiscriminately from municipal charters on the one hand and trading charters and various other sources on the other. In the joint stock companies, too, the members were "brethren", those accepted were "free of the company" or "freemen", just like the members of the innumerable medieval corporations, including the municipalities, which abounded throughout the country. Thus the East India Company, like the regulated companies, levied a special fee of admission from new members, without regard to the fact that the latter had purchased their share from a previous member. In other matters, too, the recruitment of new members corresponded to the principles prevailing in the regulated companies, with only such differences as were inevitable. Above all, new members were to be trained and brought up within the corporation and were not to be accepted haphazardly on a "capitalist" and impersonal basis [1934, 1:397].

Is it conceivable that incorporation and limited liability would have affected the terms on which an early joint-stock company could borrow? To pose the issue in this manner reveals the weakness of the capital-raising argument. Bargaining in capital markets typically takes the form of negotiated, face-to-face transactions so that the cost of bargaining is independent of the liability provisions. The interest rate is not an impersonally established price in a (Coasian) world wherein instruments are personally negotiated. The capital market will pierce the veil of limited liability in such a way as to internalize the cost of capital to a given firm. The important and predictable point is that these closely held, early joint-stock firms would have faced the same cost of capital function as the contemporaneous regulated firms. Posting of personal collateral would have been required, or the loan rate would have risen. The capital-attraction argument for the invention of the corporation is thus an inherently weak economic argument.

The scale of capital requirements does not seem to have been a barrier to the formation of early regulated companies such as the English Merchant Adventurers, the Eastland, the Levant, and the Muscovy companies. It was out of companies such as these, however, that the joint-stock form grew. The East India Company (chartered in 1600) was launched "by men who had had experience with a regulated company—the Levant Company—and the first minutes of the company were kept in the books of the Levant enterprise" (Clough and Rapp 1975, p. 152), although the Levant Company itself at times took on some of the characteristics of a joint-stock association (Scott 1951, 2:83–92). The Dutch East India Company, formed two years later, grew out of multiple partnerships and "temporary" joint-stock associations, much as the English regulated companies did. Indeed, Adam Smith's mild defense of one joint-stock company, the Hudson Bay Company, was on the grounds that such a company, "consisting of a small number of proprietors, with a moderate capital, approaches very nearly to the nature of a private copartnery, and may be capable of nearly the same degree of diligence and attention" (1937, p. 702).[11]

A final point that does not fit well with the capital-raising explanation concerns the ease with which the monopoly rights of the early firms were invaded. The following quotation from Heckscher is particularly revealing.

All this shows that the need for long-term capital was due not so much to the capital requirements of the trade itself as to the unavoidable semi-political, semi-military functions in non-European countries to which it

---

[11]Smith distrusted joint-stock companies, except in such areas as banking and insurance, as we shall discuss in the next section. An interesting counterargument to Smith's view of the early companies is given by Watts and Zimmerman (1979). They accept the fact that management and ownership were separated in the early companies, but they go on to suggest that investors had incentives to search for ways to monitor how their capital was used. Auditing consequently played a central role in facilitating the emergence of the corporation.

gave rise. This view is confirmed by the fact that the joint stock companies with legal charters always found great difficulty in protecting their trade against the "interlopers", i.e. casual and loosely organized outside enterprises; their success proved that trade itself *could* be profitably carried on by such enterprises. So long as any overseas trade was carried on outside the companies, it was a thorn in their flesh; it would not have troubled them if the interlopers had not been successful [1934, 1:406–407; italics in original].

The demand for more capital thus essentially came from the desire to suppress competition, and it is important to note here that it was easy for the interlopers to operate profitably in the same sphere as the joint-stock companies. Indeed, as Heckscher stresses, casually organized firms could operate as profitably as the joint-stock companies, a fact that would seem to suggest that the demand for capital was not a very important aspect of operating in the foreign-trade sector of those times.[12]

The property-rights argument explaining the evolution of the corporation suggests that the enhanced wealth provided by transferable ownership claims should have affected relative growth rates of organizational forms in these times.[13] Scott's emphasis upon the early and significant success of the joint-stock companies is very revealing in this respect. He estimates (1951, 1:439) that by 1720 joint-stock enterprises produced about 13 percent of English national income.

---

[12]That the interlopers were free-riding on the infrastructure of the monopoly companies is an apparent alternative hypothesis. Competitive entry and the dissipation of monopoly rents, as implied in the text, would seem to be a more viable explanation of the impact of the interlopers. A capital-intensive infrastructure was as much a policing device as a facilitator of trade for the companies.

[13]As the joint-stock form grew, institutions facilitating the floating of new issues and the trading of shares began to emerge. While the formal founding of the London Stock Exchange was not until 1773, stockbrokers and jobbers began to assemble where rich men gathered as early as the sixteenth century. Coffee houses and commodity exchanges such as the Royal Exchange (1571) or the Amsterdam Borse (1611) were popular sites (Clough and Rapp 1975, p. 155; Blum, Cameron, and Barnes 1966, p. 666). Door-to-door selling of stock shares was not unknown over the early period, as bankers had strong economic incentives to seek buyers. The institutions of stockjobbing and stock exchanges did not, of course, proceed smoothly. The South Sea Bubble of John Law burst in 1720, setting back these institutions somewhat, and the French appear to have restricted early share-trading institutions (Freedemen 1979, p. 6).

While mainly attributing the growth of the joint-stock form to the necessity for capital attraction, Scott touches upon the property-rights hypothesis when he notes the benefits of specialization that the transferability of shares permitted. He relates this point to maritime progress: "During the first half century of existence, the joint-stock company was the organization which, at each successive step, provided the requisites for the obtaining both sea-power and colonial possessions. The bravery of the privateersman and the endurance of the explorer are gratefully remembered; but, at the same time, the faith of the gentlemen and merchants, who provided the necessary capital, should not be forgotten, nor the system which had worked so smoothly on the whole and that made the co-operation of the man of action and the man of wealth possible" (1951, 1:440).

So while the two hypotheses are not mutually exclusive, the property-rights argument seems to be a more important force behind the evolution of the corporate form of business organization than the traditional demand-for-capital argument. Consequently, our point is that the demand-for-capital argument is not sufficient to explain the evolution of firms from regulated partnerships to joint-stock companies. Rather the benefits of share transferability within the mercantile cartels, expressed in terms of increased efficiency and profitability in the market for cartel management, created the necessary incentive for the emergence of the joint-stock firm and, ultimately, the modern corporation.

The legal evolution of the modern corporate form of business organization was clearly the product of centuries of adaptations. Private-firm limited liability did not receive full statutory sanction in England or the United States until well into the nineteenth century.[14] We have argued, however, that the corporation as an actual and conceptual entity had its origin in the mercantilist period. Further, our hypothesis is that share transferability as a property-rights response to profit and efficiency incentives provides an explanation superior to the traditional argument. We should like to emphasize,

---

[14]The debate generated by this legislation among professional economists over this period was both heated and protracted with (for example) N. W. Senior in favor, J. R. McCulloch vehemently opposed, and Alfred Marshall reservedly supportive of limited-liability legislation (see Amsler, Bartlett, and Bolton, forthcoming).

however, that our property-rights argument applies only at the margin. Evidence in Scott and other sources is clear that the early joint-stock companies were sometimes subject to early dissolution because of problems of managerial succession. However, the joint-stock form took root and grew relative to other forms of business organization. The evolution toward the efficiencies and increased wealth represented by tradable shares took time to work its course, and our argument is not that salable shares solved all the early joint-stock companies' problems of managerial turnover.[15] Rather we have argued that a supply-side explanation of the origin of the corporation has been ignored. Inclusion of the supply side both completes and makes more forceful the explanation of circumstances surrounding the nascence of the modern corporation.

Managerial Efficiency in the Joint-Stock Companies

A final point in our discussion of the early joint-stock companies is related to an interesting episode in the history of economic thought. Adam Smith—and he was followed in this by many other classical writers—argued that the joint-stock companies were a largely unsuccessful form of business organization, except in certain limited areas such as insurance and banking companies. He believed that they were guilty of charging noncompetitive high prices (owing to their monopoly position), of negligence, profusion, and malversation (Smith 1937, pp. 669–700). In Smith's well-known view, the inefficiency of the joint-stock company was due to the relation of its management to its owners. In a view of corporate structure close to the modern view held by Berle and Means (1932) and others, Smith saw the divorce between ownership and control—presumably not found in the private co-partnership or in the regulated companies—as creating an incentive structure wherein extreme inefficiency and managerial shirking were predictable. Further, as an example of such inefficiencies, Smith argued that joint-stock companies could seldom successfully compete against inter-

---

[15]There are testable implications of our analysis, moreover, which, with sufficient data, could be pursued. For example, corporate primogeniture should have declined over the joint-stock era, and the cost of capital to the regulated and early joint-stock companies should have been roughly equivalent.

lopers: "It is upon this account that joint stock companies for foreign trade have seldom been able to maintain the competition against private adventurers. They have, accordingly, very seldom succeeded without an exclusive privilege; and frequently have not succeeded with one. Without an exclusive privilege they have commonly mismanaged the trade. *With an exclusive privilege they have both mismanaged and confined it*" (Smith 1937, p. 100; emphasis added).

Scott (1951) challenged Smith's argument as biased, however, and presented an opposing view.[16] In Scott's view the control and internal organization of the pre-1720 joint-stock companies was far better than Smith believed, and he cites the early processes of the Royal African and Hudson's Bay companies as evidence. The early chronicles of the East India Company reveal evidence of direct managerial involvement in the company's operations. For example, officers of the company refused honoraria for managerial services, holding that the return on their equities was sufficient to compensate them for services. Scott argues, moreover, that certain controls placed on officers and directors of the company encouraged self-interested participation in matters before the firm: "In the East India company the qualification of a committee was £1,000 stock, of the governor £4,000, in the Royal African company that of an assistant was £2,000—sums which would probably be of sufficient importance to most of the adventurers in the seventeenth century to make them attentive to their duties" (Scott 1951, 1:452).

Further, Scott (1951, 1:452–453) also takes up Smith's comments about "interlopers," arguing, in contrast to Smith, that interlopers (private adventurers, smugglers) were free riders, receiving the benefits of fortifications, political interactions, and other trade infrastructure provided by the companies. Scott also seems to indicate (1951, 1:454) that interlopers were sometimes brought into the cartel, a common practice in contemporary forms of regulated monopoly. Smith's view of the interlopers as competitive entrants

[16]Scott, in fact, accuses Smith not only of almost exclusive reliance upon Anderson's *Historical and Chronological Deduction of Commerce* for his account of the joint-stock companies, but also of biased selection of examples from that work. Smith may also have utilized the very critical "Monopolies and Exclusive Companies How Pernicious to Trade" (from *Cato's Letter, or Essays on Liberty, Civil and Religious*, 1733) to develop his comments on the joint-stock argument (see the discussion in Scott 1951, 1:448–449).

seems more generally correct than Scott's characterization of them as free riders. However, this does not mean that the joint-stock firms were inefficient. It means only that it was costly to defend these monopoly rights, a fact inherent to all monopoly trading rights in these times, whether held by regulated or joint-stock firms. The enforcement or policing costs to the monopoly firms were obviously too high to exclude the interlopers completely.

From the point of view of the argument developed in this chapter, Scott was clearly on the right track in defending the efficiency with which the early joint-stock companies were managed. This was precisely the economic reason they were invented. Smith's distaste for the joint-stock company was premised upon the inevitable inefficiencies created by a divorce between owners and managers. However, Smith overstated his case. From an institutional point of view, Smith ignored the possibility of mitigating managerial disincentives by institutional-contractual arrangements. Mill (1965, pp. 138–141), for example, recognized the possibility of such contractual alternatives in his analysis of corporate property-rights arrangements. More recently, and as stressed previously in this volume, Becker and Stigler (1974) have developed an analysis in this tradition, which outlines a general theory of how malfeasance in various institutional settings can be mitigated ("pay them more and they'll steal less"). Thus, the threat of publicity, a high salary, a return as a percentage of profits, stock options, and other contractual arrangements can reduce the problem of separation of ownership from control to minimal proportions.[17] And historically, as Scott shows, accoutrements of these kinds were attached to the managerial contracts in the early joint-stock companies.

In Smith's favor, however, it may be said that managerial shirking may have simply been a red herring in his attack on monopoly. If Smith meant that monopoly chartering of the joint-stock companies by the state led to rent seeking (that is, the dissipation of expected monopoly rents) by agents for these companies, then he may be defended in his analysis of the economic inefficiency of the joint-stock companies. There is some evidence from *The Wealth of Nations*

[17]A similar situation exists in analyzing the efficiency of sharecropping arrangements (Reid 1973) or the contractual supply of local utility services (Demsetz 1968).

to support this view. Where dealing with "particular branches of commerce," Smith argues: "To establish a joint stock company . . . for any undertaking, merely because such a company might be capable of managing it successfully; or to exempt a particular set of dealers from some of the general laws which take place with regard to all their neighbours, merely because they might be capable of thriving if they had such an exemption, would certainly not be reasonable" (Smith 1937, p. 714). Thus, while Scott (1951, 1:449–452) argues that profits in early joint-stock companies were indirect evidence of good management, Smith appears to indicate that it is not the level of profits that was important, but rather the fact that they were wasted in rent-seeking activity. Rent-seeking activities by domestic cartels and international trading companies flourished throughout the entire mercantile period, as we have argued throughout this book. Viner, for example, discussed the activity of the joint-stock East India Company in the political debate surrounding the commercial clauses in the Treaty of Utrecht in 1713: "The Tories, on the other hand, came to terms with the East India Company, whereby in return for support of the endeavors of the company to preserve its monopoly privileges and to be allowed to import East Indian cloth, the latter gave financial support to the crown through loans, and to its defenders in Parliament through private bribes" (1967, p. 116). Smith does fail to recognize, however, the simple point that both the regulated companies and the joint-stock companies were state-chartered monopolies, and both were therefore subject to the charge of rent-seeking inefficiencies.

Conclusion

In the present chapter we have argued that business organization in the mercantile age was complex and evolutionary. Competitive organization began to characterize many English internal markets (as we saw in chapter 3), as it did, to some extent, French basic industry (chapter 4), while foreign-trading companies demanded and were supplied cartelization. The form and characteristics of such cartels as well as the inevitable cartel-enforcement problems were much the same as those encountered in the modern age. But from the viewpoint of rent seeking, the mercantilists behaved very rationally in the search for monopoly through regulation of *both* internal and external trade. Finally, within the mercantile rent-seeking process, the *form* of business organization was changing. The corporation grew from monopoly-inspired rent-seeking coalitions of partnerships. Indeed, there is irony in the fact that the desire to operate monopolies (regulated companies) more efficiently led to the joint-stock company, out of which the contemporary form of the competitive firm (the corporation) evolved.

6

Summation and Conclusion

And we might perhaps reply that it sometimes seems a bit
odd to us too, and that we have been making all sorts of
fumbling experiments at wider groupings and at blurring the
edges of national sovereignty; but that somehow or other,
when it comes to the point, the concept of the Nation-State,
which it has taken so many centuries to distil in the cauldron
of history, seems to have set and crystallized uncommon hard.
> Sir Dennis Robertson, *Lectures on Economic Principles*

THE conventional paradigm for analyzing mercantilism stresses the
irrationality of the mercantile social order. The mercantilists are said
to have confused power and plenty. We have argued in this study
that the essentially normative evaluation of mercantilist theory misses
much of the substance of what the mercantilists actually did. From
the viewpoint of positive economics, the mercantilists behaved quite
rationally in the pursuit of monopoly rents via the economic regulation of internal and external trade. Admittedly, both the conventional and the rent-seeking analyses of mercantilism embody the
destruction of wealth as a central concept. In the conventional paradigm wealth destruction occurs through irrational specie accumulation; in the rent-seeking paradigm it takes place through the monopolization of the economy by the state. The primary advantage that the
rent-seeking approach possesses vis-à-vis the specie-accumulation
paradigm, however, is that normally associated with positive versus
normative economics—explanatory value. Positive economics offers
a route to understanding the course of economic regulation and economic organization in the mercantile economies, while the conventional paradigm focuses mostly on the stupidity of the mercantile
writers.

The normative implications of the rent-seeking model, more-over, do not concern the irrationality of the mercantilists, but rather the welfare costs of their policies. The positive economics of rent seeking therefore concentrates on the competition for prospective rents facing demanders and suppliers of economic regulation, while the normative economics of rent seeking consists of evaluating costs to the economy of government-sponsored monopolies. Thus, in the case of English mercantilism a major point of the rent-seeking inter-pretation is that the process—including the enforcement apparatus of local regulations—helped bring about unintended institutional changes that made rent seeking and internal regulation by the cen-tral government less feasible. Under the altered institutional structure liberalism, free trade, and economic growth became viable alterna-tives. In the case of French mercantilism the rent-seeking interpreta-tion suggests a clear answer to much-debated issues concerning French economic development. That the pattern and rate of eco-nomic growth were influenced by regulatory policies of the mercan-tile administrators and that monopolization of the entire economy would retard innovation and economic growth seem to us incon-trovertible. We do not argue that rent seeking was the only force at work in impeding economic growth and industrialization and in pushing the economy toward luxury manufactures at the expense of basic productions. However, if modern studies of the social costs of monopoly and regulation are useful guides (Posner 1975; Cowling and Mueller 1978), it is not unreasonable to suggest that rent seek-ing is a very strong and heretofore unexplored explanation of the various puzzles of French economic development.

Mercantile England

The hypothesis of this book is that there were important in-stitutional changes in the rent-seeking economy of mercantilist En-gland that explain the rise of free trade on both internal and external levels. This interpretation is more robust than the standard inter-pretation of mercantilism in that it explains both the rise and fall of mercantilism with the same model. In the case of mercantile En-gland we have argued that the conventional mercantilist paradigm of power versus plenty offers no conventional means of explaining the decline of state interference. Higher cost due to uncertainty and growing private returns reduced industry demands for regulation and controls in England. All this strengthened the emergent constitutional democracy, which created conditions making rent-seeking activity on the part of both monarch and merchants more costly. When the locus of power to rent seek shifted from the monarch to Parliament via more stringent controls on the king, the costs of supplying regulation through legislative enactment rose, for reasons suggested by the theory of public choice. Lobbying costs and non-durability of laws passed due to competition within the judiciary contributed to the decline of mercantilism in England.

The competitive nature of legislatively supplied regulation, in contrast to the monarchial monopoly of an earlier period, undoubtedly reduced the net benefits from regulatory supply. A shifting institutional structure between 1540 and 1650 facilitated these developments, which were built, in turn, upon the constraints on the king, institutionalized even earlier. In addition, the inability of the monarch to enforce even simple local regulations resulted from the political structure of England and, as we have seen, from the changing cost-benefit structure to royal representatives charged with enforcement.

We have not argued that no factors other than rent seeking contributed to the decline of regulation in the post-Restoration and especially in the post-1740 period. The reform agenda for England after 1815 included a scaling down of licensing of monopolies, guild powers, and other feudal artifacts, but other changes were taking place simultaneously. Population growth, industrialization and urbanization, the almost continuous fiscal difficulties stemming from wars between 1776 and 1815, as well as other factors, may also have been influential in the ultimate demise of the old regulatory technology. After the fiscal turmoil of war, for example, the Bank of England was put back on strict convertibility in 1821, and by 1844 further restrictions cut off the treasury from any automatic access to the bank. The laws of trade and navigation were to be dismantled by Huskisson at the Board of Trade in 1825, following the Free Trade Letter of the Merchants of London in 1821.

The nature of regulation also changed somewhat in the later period to include bureaucratic and administrative enforcement machinery. Social issues were emphasized, and by mid-nineteenth century a new beginning had been made in Parliament's action in this area. A number of writers (e.g., Hartwell 1976) have commented on the origins of a professional bureaucracy and upon its critical importance for the implementation and development of social legislation in nineteenth-century England, although they have not provided a satisfying explanation for the origins of such legislation and its administration. An important exception deals with the origin of the Factory Act of 1833. The first factory act in 1802 concerned the labor of pauper children, and in 1819 Sir Robert Peel sponsored an act in Parliament that regulated hours and conditions of children's employment. Though revised in 1825 and replaced by a substitute in 1831, these acts contained very minimal provisions for enforcement. Finally, Lord Althorp's Factory Act of 1833 was drafted (under the aegis of Royal Commission Chairman Edwin Chadwick) and passed, placing controls on the employment of children in England's huge textile industry. Regarded as a landmark piece of social legislation and as one of the first important interventions into the market system in England, the Factory Act of 1833 has been subjected to both qualitative and quantitative analysis by Marvel. He concludes that his findings "suggest that this innovation in industrial regulaion was not enacted and enforced solely out of compassion for the factory children. It was, instead, an early example of a regulated industry controlling its regulators to further its own interests" (Marvel 1977, p. 402). Marvel thus describes the very same process of rent seeking in representative democracy that we have undescored in the setting of mercantile England. (The Stuart method of administering poor relief described in our chapter 3 is a good example of the effects of the administration of social policy in this era.)

Although Marvel provides evidence for a rent-seeking interpretation of one factory act, however, other forms of early nineteenth-century social controls have not received such analysis. The mode of the introduction of "neo-mercantilism" is thus an important area for future research. We have simply argued that economic incentives in the form of rivalrous rent-seeking forces were at the nexus of the decline in regulation in the sixteenth and seventeenth centuries.

The alternative hypothesis is, of course, that English intellectuals devised the case for a free economy and that their ideas had a great impact on public policy in England and, through exportation, in other European capitals (Kindleberger 1975).[1] While it is flattering to think that intellectuals affect public policy—and surely they do to some extent—it seems completely out of character for economists to think that intellectual arguments could affect real magnitudes so strongly. This is the problem with the conventional mercantilist paradigm. The mercantilists are seen as irrational specie accumulators who were routed by David Hume's specie-flow mechanism and Adam Smith's *Wealth of Nations*. The argument of this paper suggests that Hume, Smith, and all the other great free-trade intellectuals were by-standers (albeit important by-standers) in a process having its origins many years before in the changing constraints facing rent seekers in mercantile England.

Mercantile France

The pattern of mercantile rent seeking in France until the late eighteenth century was manifestly different. Absolute tax powers and ever more efficient royal enforcement at local levels permitted and supported a system of outright venality administered by an institutionalized aristocractic bureaucracy. Monarchial controls over technology further altered the cost-benefit structure of the demand for monopoly franchises by reducing the returns to production and participation in the private economy. It is easy to understand the persistence and growth of venality in France considering the degree of monopoly in the supply of franchises. Absence of meaningful rep-

[1]In an historical and quasi-Marxian interpretation of mercantilism, Magnusson (1978) emphasizes the exportation to and growth of mercantile trade policies in Sweden. Adopting the Marxian notion of the "merchant capitalist" (pp. 113–114), Magnusson explains why mercantile export policies, such as those which characterized other European countries, were so popular in Sweden: "A stratum of Swedish merchants mainly interested in exporting had already emerged and they supported a policy so manifestly designed to favour them. If mercantilism and the development of merchant capitalism are indeed closely linked, then it may be reasonably suggested that mercantilist doctrines were so rapidly accepted in Sweden, because the interests and functions of its new oligarchy resembled those of other west European countries. Heckscher, of course, rejected this view" (p. 117). An exploitative interpretation of merchant capitalism is not necessary to explain the emergence of mercantile policies of any sort. An analysis of the costs and benefits of regulatory supply and demand is relevant to any mercantile economy.

resentative institutions, or rather the conditions that would facilitate their emergence, is sufficient to explain the historical pattern.

As we have demonstrated, Louis XIII and especially Louis XIV were masters at cartel creation and enforcement. The administrative genius of a Colbert, coupled with the vast power of the crown to subdue the *parlements* and to impose absolute authority, are the proximate explanations for the incredibly vast and detailed centralized system of French mercantilism of the seventeenth and early eighteenth centuries. The forms of rent seeking in mercantile England and France were quite the same, but the difference consisted in the power to implement and to police the underlying regulations.

The ultimate question, of course, which cannot be answered fully here, revolves around the origins of the particular sets of institutions we find in the England and France of the sixteenth, seventeenth, and eighteenth centuries. That institutions were rapidly changing in both countries over this period is manifest, but it is clear that important checks (respecting taxation power, for example) were imposed upon English monarchs as early as the thirteenth century, whereas such checks were not binding in the French case until the eighteenth century. An obvious point, then, is that crucial constraints upon the power to enforce economic regulations differed greatly between France and England.

It has not been our intention in this book to present a broad social theory of why England and French institutional patterns differed over the mercantilist era. Rather, accepting institutions as given, we have analyzed English and French mercantile policies and events in positive-economic terms. We have shown that modern contributions to the theory of public choice and economic regulation provide us with explanations for episodes historians unsatisfactorily attribute to other causes.[2]

---

[2]Thus, Cole pinpoints the motive for protective regulations in the desire to encourage new industry and, indeed, utilizes the "infant-industries" argument for tariff protection as support for his argument (1939, 1:349). We would simply point out that a policy of regulating only new industries (which did not develop in mercantile France) was a convenient method of expanding the scope of a rent-seeking society. In addition, we find no evidence of significant deregulation of infant industries once they were cartelized.

Mercantile Industrial Organization

Our brief foray into the study of business organizations in the mercantile era can only serve to show the kinds of insights that may be gained from studying industrial organization during this important formative period. Most useful and relevant in the study of mercantile industrial organization are the relationships that can be observed in this period between firms and the state. In this sense there would seem to be much of value to be learned from the study of economic regulation in the mercantile economies. This is all the more true since mercantilism, conceived of as a broad process of economic regulation, seems to be a perennial state of most societies, and professional economics is just coming to grips with developing testable theories of state intervention in the economy (e.g., Stigler 1971*b*; Peltzman 1976; Pincus 1975; and Caves 1976). While the old mercantilism may have developed in a different institutional setting from the modern (monarchy versus representative democracy), it is fairly clear that the result of widespread state intervention in the economy is much the same in both cases. The old mercantilism, reinterpreted as a manifestation of man's eternal proclivities towards rent seeking, can thus serve as a useful historical laboratory for the examination of modern developments in the theory of economic regulation and the economic approach to politics. The usefulness of Demsetz's (1968) model of monopoly franchising in explaining the productive efficiency of the English regulated companies is a good example of this point. Moreover, our hypothesis concerning the origin of the corporation illustrates the old maxim that good results often spring from bad intentions. From the idea of operating monopolies more efficiently came the idea of the joint-stock companies.

Conclusion

Our theory, then, presents an explanation for the decline of mercantilism in England and for its simultaneous intensification in France. As emphasized throughout this book, mercantilism as a system of regulatory supply and demand for rent-seeking purposes has never entirely disappeared. The magnitude of controls is perhaps not

as interesting as their movement and direction, and here it is interesting to speculate on how economic controls were systematically
reduced in the English economy between 1640 and 1914. We believe that a good deal of the answer will come from further analysis
of the constraints put on rent seeking, as developed in preceding
chapters. But within any given institutional framework, we also find
individuals such as, for example, Gladstone, whose influence on economic policy spanned the middle two decades of the nineteenth century in England. His philosophy (put into practice) was one of
denying the government access to revenue-raising instruments and,
further, of raising taxes only to cover specific items of expenditure,
after which tax laws would self-destruct (Baysinger and Tollison
1980a). English fiscal conservatism of a high degree of sophistica-
tion fostered by the costs associated with parliamentary rent seeking, then, provides a potential explanation for why and how English
mercantilism subsided for so long.[3]

Thus, we have argued that the application of the modern theory
of economic regulation to the mercantile period yields new insights
into the growth and decline of mercantile restrictions. Surely our
argument would not have surprised Adam Smith, and we view it as
an extension of Smith's (admittedly) fragmentary analysis of the
rent-seeking modes of the period. As noted throughout the present
book, however, there is no dearth of arguments concerning the decline of overt mercantile policies, although the reasons for this significant episode of deregulation are largely assumed rather than explored in the literature. Credit is implicitly given to Adam Smith and
his "liberal" predecessors, who advocated the advantages of the free
and spontaneous coordination of economic activity, for making such
a forceful intellectual case for their point of view that it was trans-
lated into public policy. Our interpretation of mercantilism as a rent-
seeking society does not suggest that intellectual developments will
have much impact on public policy. We thus tend to disagree with

[3]The matter of the rise of bureaucratic neo-mercantilism is itself an interesting issue but one which is not discussed here. We would like to suggest,
however, that explanations of the emergence of a neo-mercantile bureaucracy
through public-interest arguments or as the response to "new and pressing
social problems" must be supplemented by arguments from the theory of regulation, public choice, and contractarian models of society. See, in the latter
regard, Holcombe (1980).

Keynes, who was certain "that the power of vested interests is vastly exaggerated compared with the gradual encroachment of ideas" (1936, p. 383). No matter how fine an academic scribbler Adam Smith was, we suspect that the roles of special interests and ideas were reversed in the ascension of free enterprise over mercantilism. Certainly, Smith himself characterized mercantilism correctly as a system built entirely upon self-interest.

Other types of explanations are as unlikely as the intellectual history one. For example, within the context of our rent-seeking model, the movement to free enterprise might be explained as a general process of Pareto-optimization. The inefficiencies concomitant to monopoly organization offer a range of mutually beneficial gains from exchange. Presumably consumers would offer to buy out monopolists to the net benefit of both parties. The difficulty with such a solution is the existence of prohibitively high transaction costs to consumers, which implies that monopoly and regulation will persist despite the potential social gains of ending them. Moreover, perhaps there were fewer consumers in mercantilist times, and more such Pareto-superior bargains could be struck. If this were operationally so, the movement to free enterprise from the monopolistic policies of mercantilism would be susceptible to rational explanation. This is, however, an extremely unlikely explanation of the decline of mercantilism, since the mathematics of transaction costs imply that the number of transactors must be very small before meaningful reductions in transaction costs obtain. It is therefore very likely that in mercantilist times the organizing costs to consumers would have dominated the returns from abolishing monopoly and regulation via Pareto-superior moves.

We believe, in short, that commentators on mercantilism, including Heckscher and Viner, have "overscholarized" the period. It is not that these renowned writers have not added greatly to our knowledge, but rather that they have implicitly emphasized ideas as primary causal forces of change rather than as (sometimes interesting) rationalizations based upon one's position in the rent-seeking game of income distribution. The motives of mercantile writers, as Smith cunningly indicated, should always be suspect. Heckscher has pointed out, with reference to intellectual arguments, that "there was little mysticism in the arguments of the mercantilists. . . . they did not appeal to sentiment, but were obviously anxious to find reasonable grounds for every position they adopted" (1934, 2:308).

We certainly do not disagree that writers of all persuasions sought reasonable grounds for their arguments, but we argue that these grounds in the main were a veneer over the underlying self-interested forces of the components of society.[4] The Platonic philosopher or "impartial observer," if any existed, could not have been persuasive in the absence of an institutional environment that permitted gain in the manner he supported. It is our thesis, in short, that rent-seeking engendered forces that drastically altered institutions in England, while producing in a milieu of French constraints a mercantile rigidity lasting until the nineteenth century. Our view is thus a reassertion of Smith's primitive analysis of mercantilism. It is, moreover, an elaboration of that view, in that it finds, utilizing modern theories of regulatory behavior, a crucial link between rent-seeking agents and fundamental institutional change.

[4]In a provocative paper published at the end of the nineteenth century Sir W. S. Ashley (1897) assessed the then-growing literature on free-trade "precursors" of Adam Smith. Specifically, Ashley identified the origins of the free-trade sentiments of Sir Dudley North, Sir Josiah Child, William Davenant, and Nicholas Barbon with their membership in and support of the Tory party in the late seventeenth and early eighteenth centuries. Noting a "natural connection" over the whole period, 1673–1713, between advocacy of a free-trade policy and the Tory party, Ashley argued that "it is clear that Tory writers on trade, however sensible we may suppose them, could hardly fail to have a partisan bias in favor of liberty of commerce, and that, however clear-sighted they may have been, they were likely to have their insight sharpened by party prejudice. McCulloch's explanation of North's enlightenment, that on questions of trade party interests were not directly affected, is the very opposite of truth" (1897, p. 338). Ashley proceeds, cleverly, to develop this idea and to document Tory advocacy of free trade (especially with France) as opposed to the Whig party's support of tariffs. Thus, Ashley was able to document *party* (i.e., rent-seeking) interests as dominant in the movement to free trade after the Restoration. Allied self-interested components of society (through political parties) may therefore provide the raison d'être for the views of the "moderate mercantilists" of the period. Thus, we may explain why, as Ashley reports, Josiah Child turned Tory in 1680 in order to save the privileges of the East India Company, why Barbon was one of the projectors of the Tory Land Bank, and why North eagerly served Charles II as sheriff of London during the Tory reaction (1897, p. 337). The designation of writers as "mercantile" or "liberal" based upon immediate individual interest (if, indeed, that is identifiable) must be supplemented by a study of the major tenets of party platforms and by the intraparty interactions of special-interest groups. In a mercantile context such a study would be very complex, but we believe that the general proposition raised by Ashley demands closer scrutiny.

Bibliography

Alchian, A. 1975. "Corporate Management and Property Rights." In *The Economics of Legal Relationships*, ed. H. Manne, pp. 499–510. St. Paul, Minn.: West Publishing Company.

——, and H. Demsetz. 1972. "Production, Information Costs, and Economic Organization." *American Economic Review* 62: 777–795.

Allen, W. R. 1970. "Modern Defenders of Mercantilist Theory." *History of Political Economy* 2:381–397.

Amsler, C. E., R. L. Bartlett, and C. J. Bolton. Forthcoming. "Thoughts of Some British Economists on Early Limited Liability and Corporate Legislation." *History of Political Economy*.

Ashley, W. J. 1923–1925 (first published 1906). *Introduction to English Economic History and Theory*. 2 vols. London: Longmans, Green and Company.

——. 1897. "The Tory Origins of Free Trade Policy." *Quarterly Journal of Economics* 2:335–371.

Baysinger, B., and R. D. Tollison. 1980a. "Chaining Leviathan: The Case of Gladstonian Finance." *History of Political Economy* 12:206–213.

——, and ——. 1980b. "Evaluating the Social Costs of Monopoly and Regulation." *Atlantic Economic Journal* 8:22–26.

Becker, G. 1976. "Comment." *Journal of Law and Economics* 19:245–248.

——, and G. J. Stigler. 1974. "Law Enforcement, Malfeasance, and Compensation of Enforcers." *Journal of Legal Studies* 3:1–18.

Beer, M. 1938. *Early British Economists*. London: George Allen & Unwin.

Berle, A. A., and G. Means. 1932. *The Modern Corporation and Private Property*. New York: Macmillan.

Blum, J., R. Cameron, and T. J. Barnes. 1966. *The European World*. Boston: Little, Brown and Company.

Boulenger, J. 1967. *The National History of France: The Seventeenth Century*, vol. 4, ed. F. Funk-Brentano. New York: AMS Press.

Buchanan, J. M. 1975. "Comment." *Journal of Law and Economics* 18: 903–905.

―――. 1980. "Rent Seeking and Profit Seeking." In *Toward a Theory of the Rent-Seeking Society*, ed. J. M. Buchanan, R. D. Tollison, and G. Tullock, pp. 3–15. College Station: Texas A&M University Press.

―――, and G. Tullock. 1962. *The Calculus of Consent*. Ann Arbor: University of Michigan Press.

―――, R. D. Tollison, and G. Tullock, eds. 1980. *Toward a Theory of the Rent-Seeking Society*. College Station: Texas A&M University Press.

Cameron, R., ed. 1970. *Essays in French Economic History*. Homewood, Ill.: Irwin.

Caves, R. E. 1976. "Economic Models of Political Choice: Canada's Tariff Structure." *Canadian Journal of Economics* 9:278–300.

Chalk, A. F. 1951. "Natural Law and the Rise of Economic Individualism in England." *Journal of Political Economy* 59:330–347.

―――. 1966. "Mandeville's *Fable of the Bees*: A Reappraisal." *Southern Economic Journal* 23:1–16.

Chambers, M., et al. 1974. *The Western Experience*. Vol. 2: *The Early Modern Period*. New York: A. Knopf & Co.

Clough, S. B., and R. T. Rapp. 1975. *European Economic History*. New York: McGraw-Hill Book Company.

Coats, A. W. 1957. "In Defense of Heckscher and His Idea of Mercantilism." *Scandinavian Economic History Review* 5:173–187.

Cole, C. W. 1931. *French Mercantilist Doctrines Before Colbert*. New York: Octagon Books.

―――. 1939. *Colbert and a Century of French Mercantilism*. 2 vols. New York: Columbia University Press.

―――. 1943. *French Mercantilism, 1683–1700*. New York: Columbia University Press.

Coleman, D. C. 1957. "Eli Heckscher and the Idea of Mercantilism." *Scandinavian Economic History Review* 5:3–25.

Corbbett, W. 1966 (first published 1806). *Parliamentary History of England*. Vol. 1. London: R. Bagshaw.

Cowling, K., and D. C. Mueller. 1978. "The Social Costs of Monopoly Power." *Economic Journal* 88:727–748.

Crain, W. M., and R. B. Ekelund, Jr. 1976. "Chadwick and Demsetz on Competition and Regulation." *Journal of Law and Economics* 19: 149–162.

Crain, W. M., and R. D. Tollison. 1979a. "Constitutional Change in an Interest-Group Perspective." *Journal of Legal Studies* 8:165–175.

———, and ———. 1979*b*. "The Executive Branch in the Interest-Group Theory of Government." *Journal of Legal Studies* 8:555–567.

Cunningham, W. 1968 (first published 1896–1903). *Growth of English Industry and Commerce.* 2 vols. New York: A. M. Kelley.

Davies, D. 1971. "The Efficiency of Private versus Public Firms: The Case of Australia's Two Airlines." *Journal of Law and Economics* 14:149–166.

Davis, L. E. 1980. "It's a Long Road to Tipperary, or Reflections on Organized Violence, Protection Rates, and Related Topics: The New Political History." *Journal of Economic History* 40:1–16.

Demsetz, H. 1967. "Towards a Theory of Property Rights." *American Economic Review* 57:347–359.

———. 1968. "Why Regulate Utilities?" *Journal of Law and Economics* 11:55–66.

DeRoover, R. 1944. "What Is Dry Exchange? A Contribution to the Study of English Mercantilism." *Journal of Political Economy* 52:250–266.

deVries, J. 1976. *The Economy of Europe in an Age of Crisis, 1600–1750.* Cambridge: Cambridge University Press.

Dewar, M. 1965. "The Memorandum 'For the Understanding of the Exchange': Its Authorship and Dating." *Economic History Review*: 476–487.

Douglas, G. W., and J. C. Miller. 1974. *Economic Regulation of Domestic Air Transport.* Washington: Brookings Institute.

Ehrlich, I., and R. A. Posner. 1974. "An Economic Analysis of Legal Rule Making." *Journal of Legal Studies* 3:257–286.

Ekelund, R. B., Jr., and R. F. Hébert. 1975. *A History of Economic Theory and Method.* New York: McGraw-Hill.

———, and ———. Forthcoming. "A Proto History of Franchise Bidding." *Southern Economic Journal.*

Elton, G. R. 1966. *The Tudor Revolution in Government: Administrative Changes in the Reign of Henry VIII.* Cambridge: Cambridge University Press.

Evans, G. H. 1967. "The Law of Demand: The Roles of Gregory King and Charles Davenant." *Quarterly Journal of Economics* 81:483–492.

Faith, R. L., and R. D. Tollison. 1978. "A Theory of the Supply of Occupational Regulation." Manuscript in possession of authors.

Fay, C. R. 1934. "Adam Smith, America, and the Doctrinal Defeat of the Mercantile System." *Quarterly Journal of Economics* 48:304–316.

Freedeman, C. E. 1979. *Joint-Stock Enterprise in France, 1807–1867.* Chapel Hill: University of North Carolina Press.

Furniss, E. S. 1965 (first published 1920). *The Position of the Laborer in a System of Nationalism*. New York: Augustus M. Kelley.

Grampp, W. D. 1952. "The Liberal Element in English Mercantilism." *Quarterly Journal of Economics* 66:465–501.

Haley, B. F. 1936. "Heckscher, Mercantilism." *Quarterly Journal of Economics* 50:347-354.

Hanbury, H. G. 1960. *English Courts of Law*. London: Oxford University Press.

Hartwell, R. M. 1976. "Capitalism and the Historians." In *Essays on Hayek*, ed. Fritz Machlup. New York: New York University Press.

Hayek, F. A. 1960. *The Constitution of Liberty*. Chicago: University of Chicago Press.

Heaton, C. H. 1937. "Heckscher on Mercantilism." *Journal of Political Economy* 45:370–393.

Heckscher, E. F. 1934 (first published in Swedish 1931). *Mercantilism*, trans. Mendel Shapiro. 2 vols. London: George Allen & Unwin.

———. 1955. *Mercantilism*, trans. Mendel Shapiro. 2nd. ed., rev., ed. E. G. Söderlund. 2 vols. London: George Allen & Unwin.

Herlitz, L. 1964. "The Concept of Mercantilism." *Scandinavian Economic History Review* 12:101–120.

Hinton, R. W. K. 1955. "The Mercantile System in the Time of Thomas Mun." *Economic History Review* 7:277–290.

Holcombe, R. G. 1980. "Contractarian Model of the Decline in Classical Liberalism." *Public Choice* 35:277–286.

Holdsworth, W. 1966 (first published 1903; rev. ed. first published 1922). *A History of English Law*. Vols. 1 and 4. London: Methuen and Co.

Hoselitz, B. F. 1960. "The Early History of Entrepreneurial Theory." Reprinted in *Essays in Economic Thought: Aristotle to Marshall*, ed. J. J. Spengler and W. R. Allen. Chicago: Rand McNally and Co.

Hughes, J. R. T. 1977. *The Governmental Habit: Economic Control from Colonial Times to the Present*. New York: Basic Books.

Jensen, M. C., and W. M. Meckling. 1976. "Theory of the Firm: Managerial Behavior, Agency Costs and Ownership Structure." *Journal of Financial Economics* 3:305–360.

Johnson, E. A. J. 1931. "The Mercantilist Concept of 'Art' and 'Ingenious Labour.'" *Economic History* 2:234–253.

———. 1932a. "British Mercantilist Doctrines Concerning the 'Exportation of Work' and 'Foreign-Paid Incomes'." *Journal of Political Economy* 40:750–770.

———. 1932b. "Unemployment and Consumption: The Mercantilist View." *Quarterly Journal of Economics* 46:698–719.

Keynes, J. M. 1936. *General Theory of Employment, Interest and Money*. New York: Harcourt, Brace and World.

Kindleberger, C. P. 1975. "The Rise of Free Trade in Western Europe." *Journal of Economic History* 35:20–55.

Krueger, A. O. 1974. "The Political Economy of the Rent-Seeking Society." *American Economic Review* 64:291–303.

Landes, W. M., and R. A. Posner. 1975. "The Independent Judiciary in an Interest-Group Perspective." *Journal of Law and Economics* 18: 875–901.

Lane, F. C. 1958. "The Economic Consequences of Organized Violence." *Journal of Economic History* 18:401–417.

———. 1979. *Profits from Power: Readings in Protection Rent and Violence Controlling Enterprises.* Albany: State University of New York Press.

Larson, D. A. 1970. "An Economic Analysis of the Webb-Pomerene Act." *Journal of Law and Economics* 13:461–500.

Lefebvre, G. 1947. *The Coming of the French Revolution.* Princeton: Princeton University Press.

Leoni, B. 1961. *Freedom and the Law.* Princeton: D. Van Nostrand Company.

Lewis, P. S. 1968. *Later Medieval France.* New York: St. Martin's Press.

Lough, J. 1960. *An Introduction to Eighteenth Century France.* London: Longmans, Green and Co.

———. 1969. *An Introduction to Seventeenth Century France.* New York: David McKay, Co.

McCormick, R. E., and R. D. Tollison. 1980. "Wealth Transfers in a Representative Democracy." In *Toward a Theory of the Rent-Seeking Society,* ed. J. M. Buchanan, R. D. Tollison, and G. Tullock, pp. 293–313. College Station: Texas A&M University Press.

Macfarlane, A. 1978. *The Origins of English Individualism: The Family, Property and Social Transition.* New York: Cambridge University Press.

Magnusson, L. 1978. "Eli Heckscher, Mercantilism, and the Favorable Balance of Trade." *Scandinavian Economic History Review* 26:103–127.

Maitland, F. W. 1908. *Constitutional History of England.* Cambridge: Cambridge University Press.

———. 1957. *Selected Historical Essays of F. W. Maitland,* ed. Helen M. Cam. Cambridge: Cambridge University Press.

———, and F. C. Montague. 1915. *A Sketch of English Constitutional History.* New York: G. O. Putnam's Sons.

Maloney, M. T., and R. E. McCormick. 1980. "Environmental Quality Regulation." Manuscript in possession of authors.

Marris, R., and D. C. Mueller. 1980. "The Corporation and Competition." *Journal of Economic Literature* 18:32–63.

Marshall, T. H. 1935. "Review of Heckscher's *Mercantilism.*" *Economic Journal* 14:716–719.

Marvel, H. P. 1977. "Factory Regulation: A Reinterpretation of Early English Experience." *Journal of Law and Economics* 20:379–402.

Meiners, R. E., J. S. Mofsky, and R. D. Tollison. 1979. "Piercing the Veil of Limited Liability." *Delaware Journal of Corporation Law* 4:351–367.

Mettam, R. 1977. *Government and Society in Louis XIV's France.* London: Macmillan.

Mill, J. S. 1965 (reprint of 1909 ed.; first published 1848). *Principles of Political Economy*, ed. W. Ashley. New York: Augustus M. Kelley.

Moote, A. L. 1971. *The Revolt of the Judges.* Princeton: Princeton University Press.

Morris, C. T. 1957. "Some Neglected Aspects of Sixteenth Century Economic Thought." *Explorations in Entrepreneurial History* 9:160–171.

Nef, J. U. 1968 (first published 1940). *Industry and Government in France and England, 1540–1640.* New York: Russell and Russell.

Nichols, W. M. 1941. *Imperfect Competition within the Agricultural Industries.* Ames: Iowa State College Press.

North, D. C. 1978. "Structure and Performance: The Task of Economic History." *Journal of Economic Literature* 16:963–978.

———. 1979. "A Framework for Analyzing the State in Economic History." *Explorations in Economic History* 16:249–259.

———, and R. P. Thomas. 1973. *The Rise of the Western World.* Cambridge: Cambridge University Press.

Peltzman, S. 1976. "Toward a More General Theory of Regulation." *Journal of Law and Economics* 2:211–240.

Pincus, J. J. 1975. "Pressure Groups and the Pattern of Tariffs." *Journal of Political Economy* 83:757–778.

Plucknett, T. F. 1948. *A Concise History of the Common Law.* London: Butterworth and Co.

Pollock, F., and F. W. Maitland. 1895. *The History of English Law before the Time of Edward I.* Vols. 1 and 2. Cambridge: Cambridge University Press.

Posner, R. A. 1971. "Taxation by Regulation." *Bell Journal of Economics and Management Science* 2:22–50.

———. 1974. "Theories of Economic Regulation." *Bell Journal of Economics and Management Science* 5:335–358.

———. 1975. "The Social Costs of Monopoly and Regulation." *Journal of Political Economy* 83:807–827.

Power, E. 1941. *The Wool Trade in English Medieval History.* London: Oxford University Press.

Priest, G. L. 1975. "The History of the Postal Monopoly in the United States." *Journal of Law and Economics* 18:33–80.

Reid, J. D. 1973. "Sharecropping as an Understandable Market Response: The Post-Bellum South." *Journal of Economic History* 33:106–130.

Robertson, D. 1957. *Lectures on Economic Principles*. Vol. 1. London: Staples Press.

Roehl, R. 1976. "French Industrialization: A Reconsideration." *Explorations in Economic History* 13:233–281.

Roy, P. 1943. "The Mercantilist View of Money in Relation to Public Finance." *Indian Journal of Economics* 23:257–270.

Rudé, G. F. 1964. *The Crowd in History: A Study of Popular Disturbances in France and England 1730–1848*. New York: John Wiley.

Schmoller, G. 1897. *The Mercantile System and Its Historical Significance*. New York: Macmillan.

Schumpeter, J. A. 1954. *History of Economic Analysis*. New York: Oxford University Press.

Scott, W. R. 1951 (first published 1912). *The Constitution and Finance of English, Scottish, and Irish Joint-Stock Companies to 1720*. 2 vols. New York: Peter Smith.

Scoville, W. C. 1960. *The Persecution of Huguenots and French Economic Development, 1680–1720*. Berkeley and Los Angeles: University of California Press.

See, H. 1927. *Economic and Social Conditions in France during the Eighteenth Century*. New York: Alfred Knopf.

Smith, A. 1937 (first published 1776). *The Wealth of Nations*, ed. E. Cannan. New York: Random House.

Stigler, G. J. 1951. "The Division of Labor Is Limited by the Extent of the Market." *Journal of Political Economy* 59:185–193.

———. 1964. "A Theory of Oligopoly." *Journal of Political Economy* 72:44–61.

———. 1968. "Price and Non-Price Competition." *Journal of Political Economy* 76:149–154.

———. 1971*a*. "Smith's Travels on the Ship of State." *History of Political Economy* 3:265–277.

———. 1971*b*. "The Theory of Economic Regulation." *Bell Journal of Economics and Management Science* 2:3–21.

———, and C. Friedland. 1962. "What Can Regulators Regulate? The Case of Electricity." *Journal of Law and Economics* 5:1–23.

Tawney, R. H., ed. 1958. *Studies in Economic History: The Collected Papers of George Unwin*. London: Royal Economic Society Reprint.

———, and E. Power. 1924. *Tudor Economic Documents*. Vols. 1, 2, and 3. London: Longmans, Green and Co.

Taylor, H. 1898. *The Origin and Growth of the English Constitution*. Part 2. Boston: Houghton, Mifflin and Company.

Tollison, R. D. 1978. "An Historical Note on Regulatory Reform." *Regulation* 2:46–49.

Tullock, G. 1967. "The Welfare Costs of Tariffs, Monopolies, and Theft." *Western Economic Journal* 5:224–232.

————. 1978. "The Backward Society: Static Inefficiency, Rent Seeking, and the Rule of Law." Manuscript in possession of author.

————. 1980. "Efficient Rent Seeking." In *Toward a Theory of the Rent-Seeking Society*, ed. J. M. Buchanan, R. D. Tollison, and G. Tullock, pp. 97–112. College Station: Texas A&M University Press.

Tuma, E. H. 1971. *European Economic History*. New York: Harper & Row.

Vaughn, K. I. 1980. *John Locke: Economist and Social Scientist*. Chicago: University of Chicago Press.

Viner, J. 1930. "English Theories of Foreign Trade Before Adam Smith." Parts 1 and 2. *Journal of Political Economy* 38:249–301, 404–457.

————. 1967 (first published 1937). *Studies in the Theory of International Trade*. New York: Augustus M. Kelley.

Wagner, D. O. 1935. "Coke and the Rise of Economic Liberalism." *Economic History Review* 6:30–44.

Watts, R., and J. Zimmerman. 1979. "The Markets for Independence and Independent Auditors." Manuscript in possession of authors.

Williamson, O. E. 1976. "Franchise Bidding for Natural Monopolies— In General and with Respect to CATV." *Bell Journal of Economics* 7:73–104.

Wolfe, M. 1972. *The Fiscal System of Renaissance France*. New Haven: Yale University Press.

Index